D1481541

Everyone Needs Attention

Other Redleaf Press Books by Tamar Jacobson

"Don't Get So Upset!": Help Young Children Manage Their Feelings by Understanding Your Own

Perspectives on Gender in Early Childhood (Editor)

HELPING YOUNG CHILDREN THRIVE

Everyone Needs Attention

Tamar Jacobson, PhD

Redleaf Press®
www.redleafpress.org
800-423-8309

Published by Redleaf Press
10 Yorkton Court
St. Paul, MN 55117
www.redleafpress.org

© 2018 by Tamar Jacobson

All rights reserved. Unless otherwise noted on a specific page, no portion of this publication may be reproduced or transmitted in any form or by any means, electronic or mechanical, including photocopying, recording, or capturing on any information storage and retrieval system, without permission in writing from the publisher, except by a reviewer, who may quote brief passages in a critical article or review to be printed in a magazine or newspaper, or electronically transmitted on radio, television, or the Internet.

First edition 2018
Cover design by Charles Rue Woods
Cover photograph by Tomwang112, Getty Images/iStockphoto
Interior design by Jim Handrigan and Douglas Schmitz
Typeset in Utopia
Printed in the United States of America
25 24 23 22 21 20 19 18 1 2 3 4 5 6 7 8

Library of Congress Cataloging-in-Publication Data
Names: Jacobson, Tamar, author.
Title: Everyone needs attention : helping young children thrive / Tamar Jacobson, PhD.
Description: St. Paul, MN : Redleaf Press, [2018] | Includes bibliographical references.
Identifiers: LCCN 2018012943 (print) | LCCN 2018021111 (ebook) | ISBN 9781605545882 (ebook) | ISBN 9781605546551 (pbk. : alk. paper)
Subjects: LCSH: Attention-seeking. | Child psychology. | Parenting.
Classification: LCC BF637.A77 (ebook) | LCC BF637.A77 .J33 2018 (print) | DDC 153.1/532--dc23
LC record available at https://lccn.loc.gov/2018012943

Printed on acid-free paper

I dedicate this book to my father, Ezekiel Israel,
who loved his "Tamarika" gently,
and
to Stephen Stelzer,
who helped me to feel and heal.

Contents

Acknowledgments

AT RIDER UNIVERSITY, Department of Teacher Education faculty members get together to share ideas at regular Research Tuesday meetings. One of my presentations during such a meeting became the basis for this book. I am grateful to the faculty at that time for their warm collegiality and interest in my work.

All throughout the writing of this book, I thought about the many teachers who worked with me at the University at Buffalo Child Care Center during my eleven-year tenure as director. They stood up to the challenge of relearning the teaching script and participated in our experiment to do without punishments and rewards as well as silly-smiling Disney characters. Some learned to enjoy carrying children on their backs, and they loved and educated the children in our care with endless devotion and an emerging curriculum. I am enormously grateful for every one of these caring and gifted educators.

In 2001, at the NAEYC conference in Anaheim, California, Danny Miller wandered into my presentation called "The Anti-Bias Curriculum: Looking Back and Thinking Forward." There were about a hundred people in the room that day, so I didn't notice anyone in particular. One week later, Danny sent me an email. As an acquisitions editor for Heinemann, he was looking for early childhood authors and had stumbled upon me that day at the conference. In his email, he asked if I would like to write a book on the topic of my presentation. I stared at the computer screen in disbelief. It felt as if I had won some kind of lottery. I felt discovered! It is impossible to describe my mixed feelings of excitement and anxiety as I replied, eagerly agreeing to write a proposal for a book I had been thinking of for many years. A couple of weeks later, I flew to Washington, DC, from Buffalo, New York, to meet him. Out of that historic (for me) meeting, my first book was born: *Confronting Our Discomfort: Clearing the Way for Anti-Bias in Early Childhood* (2003).

Four years later, Danny encouraged and inspired me to start my first blog and has been a constant supporter of my writing for the past twelve years. Danny has given me the perfect support and encouragement I needed for writing right from my heart and from the depths of emotional memories in my brain. In short, Danny gave me the opportunity to find my author's voice. I will be forever grateful to him. Imagine my delight when the wonderful editorial team at Redleaf Press, headed by David Heath, suggested Danny edit this book, *Everyone Needs Attention*. I mean, just how lucky can one gal get?

More than a decade ago, my husband and I relocated from Buffalo to Philadelphia and were fortunate to find our beautiful Craftsman home in the neighborhood of Mount Airy, right in the midst of a diverse and progressive community. Quickly we befriended a number of intellectual and compassionate people. We had no option not to, for they opened up their arms, hearts, and homes to us in times of joy and especially in periods of sorrow. A number of people from this vibrant and caring community were supportive of me through the writing of this book. They walked and talked with me and listened to my endless stories, concerns, and angst. More importantly, though, they validated and believed in me. Thank you, especially to Betsy Teutsch and Helen Feinberg.

My husband, Tom, has been with me throughout my acquiring a PhD and writing all my books. Over the years, he has been willing to be grist for my writing and presentation mill in my countless examples taken from our relationship. He has endless patience as he listens to my reading aloud what I write, as well as a keen editorial eye when he volunteers to read my pages. I am grateful that he has hung in there with me as we constantly learn how to live in relationship together year in and year out.

Finally, some special thanks go to sweet, little four-month-old Benya, who allowed me to practice caregiving and relationship on him in the long, hot afternoons during most of the summer while I was writing this book.

Preface

Pay Attention to Children with an Open Heart

When a person doesn't have gratitude, something is missing in his or her humanity. A person can almost be defined by his or her attitude toward gratitude. —*Elie Wiesel (2000)*

As I was writing this book, my mother passed away just a week short of her hundredth birthday. While going through the grief process, I uncovered a series of repressed emotions about my relationship with her that seemed all the more relevant and helpful as I was exploring issues around children and their need for attention.

Indeed, somewhere there inside all my stifled emotions was the feeling that my mother would, at the end, acknowledge or validate me in some profound way. I did not expect an apology for the way she had excluded and shunned me time and again since I was a young child, although in the end I think I still might have held out for one. I did not expect to be acknowledged or validated, although I think I might have been holding out for that as well. These feelings were submerged—buried so deep in my psyche that I was shocked when I finally allowed myself to feel them. The pain of them would rise up suddenly in the most unexpected moments starting soon after her burial in the little village of Michmoret in Israel, where she had lived for almost half a century.

When I returned home after her funeral and the *shivah*, I was numb. Shocked. My increasingly ill mother had defied death for five years, and I found it difficult to imagine a world without her. She had been such an enormous presence and influence in my life, and I had yearned for her love and acknowledgment for as long as I could remember. As the days drifted by, emotions started to poke through. I began to realize that during the last weeks that I sat with her, played music I thought she might enjoy listening to, and stroked her hair and hands, telling her I loved her, I was holding out for a sign. Some sort of recognition of my devotion and love—a smile, perhaps, a holding on to *my* hand. Something. Anything. It never came, even though I heard from others that she had turned toward them and smiled in a way that seemed intentional. Even as we laid her body to rest in the small village cemetery, I realized that like a child, I was waiting for her to rise up out of the grave and exclaim, "Hey! Tamar—I loved you—don't ever forget that!"

And when, finally, emotions started to push through my crumbling, numbed state, they were of sadness and anger at not having been acknowledged in any way, even at the very end. While it has been excruciating at times, I have been making many connections with my grief and the subject of this book—how much children (and people of all ages) desperately need the attention of the adults in their lives. These feelings from childhood never really leave us; they return over and over again in different forms and at unexpected moments. This increased awareness of my own experience accentuates for me just how important it is to give our youngest children the feeling that they are wanted, loved, noticed, and worthwhile—just by virtue of who they are and what they have to contribute. Nothing is as painful as having our love rejected or ignored.

Giving or withholding of attention is really all about relationship—it is not an act on its own. It is connected to all the complex feelings we have toward one another. As an adult, I understand that many of the times I was ignored, criticized, or excluded had nothing to do with who I am or even what I had done. They had everything to do with my mother's insecurities, her feelings of disappointment and frustration about her own life, and her relationships with her mother, husbands, and others. However, as a child, I couldn't be aware of all of that, and I needed her to be there for me emotionally.

As my grief starts to feel manageable, I understand more and more about my mother and who she was as a person—charismatic and strong-willed, and someone who went through quite a lot in her own life of nearly a hundred years. I realize some of the great things I learned from her, including my love of gardening, reading, and music. I am able to balance all that with my sadness at losing her, the lost hope of her ever acknowledging me in the ways that I craved, and the pain of what I yearned for from her as a child, and even as her adult daughter.

One morning, I received an email from a friend, who wrote:

> Good luck with the writing. I hope it is cathartic. I am sure that your plumbing the depths of memory will be redemptive—in helping so many others to pay attention to children, with an open heart.

I was grateful for these words because of how succinctly they captured the essence of this book. I sense, as I head toward full retirement in a couple of years, that this might even be the last book I write for educators of young children, and it seems to be the hardest one for me, mainly because this is a subject that is even nearer to my heart than the subjects of my other books. To be honest, this is a subject that breaks my heart because of how painful it is for me to think about the times I have seen adults treat children with disdain, humiliating and shaming them, when all the children really needed from them at the time was compassion and attention. And because compassionate relationship, acknowledgment, and validation is what I so craved when I was a child, these experiences tap into my own emotional experience, and I feel for children in our care even more.

When I mentioned to my therapist how grieving my mother is so much more difficult than I imagined, he responded, "You are not grieving as much for your mother as you are for your life—your childhood life where your feelings were stifled." I sense a kind of release as each memory presents itself, seemingly out of nowhere, and I weep it out of me. An unburdening follows as I allow myself to experience the yearning I held in for so long.

My friend's words help me realize how important this book is for me. It feels like it has been residing in my brain all my life. I have no illusions that it will change the world, or even sell very well—most education books don't! But, really, if it helps even *one* adult pay attention to *one* child with an open heart, I will feel satisfied. I know that when I was young, I would have followed people to the ends of the earth if I felt, even for a brief moment, that they related to me—accepted me with compassion and understanding—and I am certain that such moments that came from the kindness of strangers over the course of my childhood saved me and nurtured my resilience.

In a weird way, I am grateful to my mother too. I mean this most sincerely. She needed me emotionally between my ages of seven and eighteen, and even though I suffered by putting my needs away and placing hers front and center, I learned to care for someone other than myself. I learned a great deal about empathy and compassion from a very early age: whether it was through carrying away pots of her vomit at the age of seven when she was pregnant with my younger brother; wiping her forehead with a cool cloth when she was tormented and crying, anxious about my stepfather leaving her; listening to her early-morning stories about whether sex had been good or bad the night before with my stepfather, or to her weeping and fretting about my older siblings for this or that; or actively listening while she complained about the servants, family members, her friends, and all the other people who she believed were "out to get her"—the list is endless.

I learned early on to put aside whatever it was I was doing, thinking, or feeling and to just be present for her. I learned to silently listen and hold her in my heart. And many, many times, even as a child, I would hold or hug her to comfort her and try to assure her that everything would be all right. Indeed, I learned mothering from mothering my mother! Little did I know that I was honing skills necessary for empathy and compassion that would later be crucial as an adult for my work with children, teachers, and families. Although my service to my mother was not met with gratitude from her, I learned to be grateful for any crumb of acknowledgment that would come my way.

I realized this most acutely just a few years ago when my mother was bedridden in her late nineties and was seated in a chair in my sister's house when I was visiting. She was complaining because her fingernails and toenails hadn't been cut in a while. I immediately asked for clippers from my sister and tenderly and carefully trimmed her fingernails. Then I got on my knees at her feet and clipped her toenails. All the while, I was trying to be gentle because she expressed anxiety about having me do this. I spoke quietly to her and stroked her when I could. When I was done, I sat back on the couch. My mother was still for a moment, staring ahead, and then called out to my sister, "Tell the pedicurist I don't need her!" I stared at her and thought: "Wow! Not even a tiny thank-you." My entire childhood flashed before my eyes. No gratitude for anything I had ever done for her. It was a revelation. At that moment, I felt deep sadness for my mother. Gratitude lifts us up out of bitterness and sorrow, and without it she was, as it happened, left with so much unnecessary misery when she died.

Of course, as an older woman with life experience and knowledge about child development and the care and education of young children, I now understand that I did what I did that day in the hopes my mother would love and appreciate me. Yes. *I did it for her attention.* So while I learned to care for another with empathy and compassion, I also learned to make myself invisible and to stifle any feelings about how much I longed to be mothered myself. Perhaps now that I am in my late sixties, I can be proud of what I have accomplished in spite of all that stuff, learn more about my own self-worth, and, finally, change my emotional life script for good (Jacobson 2008). Hopefully, too, as I release these memories and learn to mother myself more and more, I will find a balance in helping others with being present for me as well. And more importantly, I can give to children and adults what I wished I had received.

Introduction

Lessons from Years of Caring about Young Children

WHENEVER I ENTER A CLASSROOM as a teacher, all that is about and within me accompanies me into the room. As I apply theory into practice, the ways that I behave or interact with children and their families are influenced by my life experiences as well as my knowledge about child development. Indeed, I cannot separate teacher Tamar from personal me. Everything about how I came to be me affects my worldview about children.

All kinds of facts about my life affect the way I perceive children and their families and how I interact with them: The fact that I am the fourth of five of my mother's children makes me feel like almost the youngest and everything that comes with that label. That my father was not the same as my siblings' father means I always feel excluded and long to belong. That I suffered emotional abuse during my childhood makes me less confident and trusting. That I am a woman makes me aware of the power struggles between the genders. That I was brought up Jewish and atheist affects how I experience spirituality. That during my childhood I grew up in Africa as a white, Jewish girl makes me aware of my white, privileged background and the urgency of diversity acceptance. That as a young adult I spent twenty years teaching makes me understand what it is like to be in a classroom with young children. That I am a mother makes me able to put myself in parents' shoes. That I married and divorced more than once makes me capable of understanding different family styles and configurations. That I had one son and was at times a single parent makes me aware of the emotional challenges and financial struggles of being a single parent. That I put myself through school at the age of forty means I know that it is never too late to accomplish anything if I put my mind to it. That ever since I can remember I learned to go it alone and not to expect acknowledgment for my accomplishments, academic or personal, makes me independent but also makes me struggle with reaching out for help.

Somehow, from all of those experiences, I developed perspectives that make me believe that the quality of our relationships with young children is not only critical for their emotional health and well-being but also affects children for the rest of their lives, both personally and academically. As simple as it sounds, *caring about young children* has become one of my most basic pedagogical principles and the cornerstone of my philosophy of education. I think that for some people the phrase *caring about young children* sounds a bit trite or irrelevant to proclaim. Don't we all care about young children? However, when I use these words, they have a specific meaning for me, and they have evolved out of what I went through growing up and how I made connections between those lessons and what I later learned about child development and appropriate practice. In other words, for me *caring about young children* means, first and foremost, concern for their *emotional* well-being. Therefore, in whatever I set out to do, whether it is read a story, design the physical environment, observe and assess, create an emerging, play-based curriculum, or teach mathematics, concern for children's emotional well-being is my primary focus.

The Importance of Relationship

Ever since I was a preschool and kindergarten teacher in Israel, I have been curious about how self-reflection affects my relationships with young children and their families (Jacobson 2008). During the past several years, research about the effects of our relationships with children on brain development has confirmed what I always understood intuitively: what we do with very young children lasts forever (Jacobson 1999). One of my tasks as an early childhood teacher educator is to help teachers understand how their relationships with young children affect the development of emotional memory templates in the brain (Szalavitz and Perry 2010). Indeed, the entire focus of my work and writing is about understanding how our emotions or biases affect our interactions and behaviors with young children and their families (Jacobson 2003, 2008, 2010).

Meaningful, loving relationships with adults are crucial for attachment and young children's emotional development (Gerhardt 2004; Jacobson 2006; Karr-Morse and Wiley 1997; Perry 2007). Indeed, the literature on this subject is a confirmation of what I have been uncovering about *my own* emotional development and how *I* feel. It helps me understand how and why I might have struggled with many of my relationships over these past six decades, and on a professional level, it is connected to helping me understand and improve my relationships with young children, families, and teachers.

One of the ways we can be more intentional in our interactions and behaviors with children and families is to learn how to research the self, which I wrote about in one of my previous books:

> We can start becoming aware of the inner emotional life that we have developed since we were young children by observing our interactions and noticing the types of behaviors or emotional situations with children that make us most

> uncomfortable. Making a detailed and deliberate account of our inner feelings is what I would like to call "researching the self." In other words, I am suggesting we become observers of ourselves! Or put another way, we become researchers of our own emotional lives. When we observe and notice, in a deliberate way, our own interactions or what makes us uncomfortable, we are, in fact, collecting data about ourselves—just as researchers do. (Jacobson 2008, 108)

Understanding what makes us tick emotionally is another way to *know thyself*, and this awareness helps us become more professional about the choices we make in our interactions with children and families. It directly affects our intentionality. Gloria Steinem (1993) talks about *a revolution within* and suggests that emotional self-reflection is critical to our ability to change old patterns of behavior as we strive for social justice. She suggests that only when we become conscious of our early childhood memories are we then able to change patterns of behavior we learned when we were very young.

The importance of our relationships with young children cannot be stressed enough. Lately there has been much discussion and debate about using standardized testing and teacher accountability as ways to improve children's academic achievements. A few years ago, I watched an eighteen-minute comedy segment with John Oliver (2015) about the negative aspects of standardized testing and how this testing is, in fact, not effective in improving American students' academic achievements. While I was both amused and shocked by the speculations and conclusions Oliver came to in his comedic rant, one piece in particular troubled me to the core. He reported that teachers in Ohio are given instructions about what to do if a child vomits all over the test papers from fear.

The audience laughed out loud about such a thing occurring. My dismay came from the fact that children's fears about test taking have become so commonplace that the administrators have worked out procedures for dealing with the physical manifestations of that emotion. Indeed, what seems to be lacking from the national discussion about standardized testing and academic achievement is anything about the importance of the relationships between adults and children in schools. While everyone is concerned with cognitive development and the proof of its success, children's emotions are usually ignored, and the emotional lives of the adults who work with them are neglected even more. For example, I wonder what teachers might feel when their students are so frightened of test taking that they throw up all over the papers!

I have been focused on children's emotional development and well-being from the beginning of my early adulthood. Indeed, one of the main lessons I have learned about teaching young children is that kindness and compassion are essential for developing quality relationships. Not everyone will agree with all my ideas. That is as it should be! After all, they have evolved through *my* education and experience. I hope, however, that they will provide another option to consider while working with young children.

Engaging in Reflective Practice

State and federal standards used to require teachers to cultivate certain attitudes toward reflective thinking, such as open-mindedness, wholeheartedness, and responsibility for facing the consequences (Jacobson 2003, 2008). Much of the research about reflective practice looks at teachers' ability to assess a situation and make sense out of the experience. Reflective practice is not new. John Dewey wrote about it many years ago, as did Donald Schön (Jacobson 2003, 2008). Indeed, self-awareness assists teachers in becoming more intentional in their classroom practice. I wonder how teachers can be effective if they are not in touch with their own emotional development, since our interventions in emotional situations are crucial in helping children acquire a positive emotional self-identity (Jacobson

2003, 2008). Teachers who reflect on how and why they feel the way they do are in a better position to understand their interactions with others. And if we are not aware of what frightens or concerns us, what causes us anxiety, or what our own emotional limitations are, we will find it much more difficult to be as supportive with the children in our care as we would like. We might, in fact, unintentionally shame a child the way we were humiliated as children.

Marilou Hyson (2004) tells us that children's *emotional development is too important to be left to chance.* I have heard Bruce Perry (2007) say time and again that we have the choice to develop humane children starting from their earliest years by giving them strong, repetitive, positive emotional memories. How do we do that if some of us did not experience humane treatment growing up? Teachers' emotional development is too important to be left to chance. In the late 1950s and 1960s, teacher educators suggested that preparing teachers should include a development of awareness about their emotional lives, that human emotional qualities are at the core of teaching, and that the very behavior of teachers is a product of their emotional self-identity (Jacobson 2003). The literature from that time focused on teachers' emotional development, whereas these days there is much less discussion about this type of self-reflection.

In my first two books (2003, 2008), I shine a light on and discuss the research about reflective practice in teacher education. However, I believe there is an area of reflective practice that needs further exploration: one that focuses on "knowing thyself" emotionally and psychologically. It takes courage to confront our emotions and make connections between how we were treated when we were young and how that affects our behaviors and interactions as adults caring for young children. I realize that this is more challenging than the other types of reflective practice.

Facing ourselves critically is never easy and may even be considered uncomfortable for many people. For example, for many years, with the help of a professional therapist, I worked through some of my own early childhood issues. I found myself having to confront feelings of low self-worth and anger toward my parents, whom I loved. This was challenging and also painful at times. However, once I came to terms with my psychological and emotional development, I was able to enhance the quality of my life considerably and, more importantly, improve my interactions, behaviors, and relationships with others.

Everyone Needs Attention

In 2008 I wrote about children seeking attention *only* when they feel unloved or unwanted. I made a brief mention of this topic in a chapter about discipline, suggesting that this might be a problem for teachers. Little did I realize how complex and important a topic it is in our interactions with children. I wrote:

> Achieving the type of attention [children] deserve is elusive to them. . . . This is yet another area where children may develop ways to gain control over their lives. Attention seeking can take on many different forms, and often it is through negative and self-destructive behaviors. When teachers tell me, "He's just doing that [whatever it is] for attention," my reply is usually something like, "Then, find many constructive ways to give him attention! If he is doing other unacceptable-to-you types of things for attention, he still needs attention!" It is at those very moments when children need our attention that I see teachers choosing to ignore them as an effective strategy. In other words, we take away from them what they need so desperately from us. (Jacobson 2008, 127)

Since my book came out, the subject of children wanting attention has come up over and over again as one of the key topics of concern during my keynote speeches and workshops about discipline for teachers and administrators at regional, state, and national levels. Attention seeking is seen as misbehavior, just as I considered it to be almost a decade ago, and whenever I now suggest giving children the attention they need, it is often interpreted as reinforcement of bad behavior. Most behavior management experts advise against giving children too much attention because they say it will reinforce children's bad behaviors when they need to learn how to *self-regulate*. Do we always have to withhold attention in order for children to self-regulate? Or could we reconsider and support them while they learn to become independent of us? In other words, instead of withholding our attention or constantly setting conditions for children to receive our approval, could we try out more constructive responsiveness?

In this book, I focus on how we manage our emotions, specifically when children seek our attention, and include a chapter to help teachers reflect specifically about how they sought out attention when they were young. I question when and why teachers perceive children's need for attention as something negative—something in the way of their learning or understanding of human relationships. Surely it comes from the way we were treated as young children, from the repetitive subtle and not-so-subtle condemnation of the ways we sought attention from significant adults in our lives, when we were thought of as too whiny, needy, brazen, or outspoken.

These days, self-regulation has become an overused catchphrase that is thrown into any conversation about children who seek our attention. Self-regulation, while important for teaching children limits and the behavioral norms of our society, also requires small children to go it alone emotionally and learn not to reach out or lean on those adults who care for and educate them. There has to be a balance between needing attention and learning to delay gratification, but this can be taught through connection and relationship, not through exclusion and punishment. Child development is just that—developing, evolving into the adults we will one day become. As adults, we can share what we learned with children in our care with love, in friendship, and with guidance and support—or we can admonish and scold with punishment and harsh rationalism. The choice is ours. We don't have to repeat the pain we experienced. We can change and try something different that we might not be familiar with but nevertheless would have liked to experience when we were children—something that we really have always yearned for all along. Our choice to change the way we think about giving attention becomes a gift not only to the children in our care but to future generations, and ultimately this change will benefit us as adults too.

More than a year ago, I was invited, along with many other early childhood professional development experts and teacher educators, to train preschool teachers with the New York City Department of Education for their *Pre-K for All* program. As I was writing this book, one of those teachers who had participated in my training section sent me a message through Facebook. He wrote that he was thinking about me because he had just read my book *"Don't Get So Upset!"* (2008). He wrote:

> The book and the hard work within has such resonance for me—being a male pre-K teacher who has issues around self-assertion and anger. Reading your personal history was much like looking at my own. . . . My transition into teaching was tumultuous, and I am still working on unpacking and letting go of some unhelpful feelings, and I just wanted to let you know your writing, your existence is a key part of my moving forward.

I am always delighted to hear from people who take seriously the challenging, joyful work of teaching young children. Plus, I wanted to hear what he thought of the book and how it might have been useful for him. I responded to him, saying that I was pleased to hear from him and wondering what he thought of my book, and asked if he would tell me more about himself. He replied:

> I'll start with my sole criticism, which is actually not a criticism at all. I think teachers who pick up your book looking for quick fixes and reliable scripts to follow in high-pressure situations will be sorely disappointed. But I believe that is one of the salient points of your book. On to what I loved! The book reads like what I imagine it must be like to take one of your college courses. It's filled with personal anecdotes and jam-packed with references for further study. The core provocations like the personal ethnography demand deep reflection. The reader is only going to get something meaningful out of the book if they do the work. And you engender this deep reflection (and action) by leading with vulnerability, humor, and forgiveness. This was the most powerful part of the book for me; some of the ways you described your psychology reminded me so much of my own. Particularly when you describe yourself as someone who has lived their life "in and out of confidence" and "attractiveness."

I was pleased with his description of the book, especially the part where he wrote, "The reader is only going to get something meaningful out of the book if they do the work." The work. Do the work. I hear you groan, "What, more work? Don't I have enough to do already?" I get it—we early childhood folk are always asking you to do just a little more to improve yourself and your teaching/caregiving. We instruct you how to talk to children, tell you what disciplinary strategies to use, and encourage you to read more and more. The work is endless. However, what I am asking you to do here is to get to know *yourself* better. I am inviting you to learn about how you became who you are and what and who influenced and affected you, but, most of all, how the interactions with adults in your childhood made you feel—especially when you needed attention from them.

I am inviting you into a space we often leave unexamined because we might have put aside emotions that were too uncomfortable to deal with when we were children. I am doing this because I believe it will be helpful for you in your emotional work with children, but, more than that, it might be beneficial for you to enrich your relationships, professionally and personally. When I become more aware of how I tick emotionally, I am able to be more intentional and have more options in choosing how to behave—not only with children but, in fact, with everyone in my life. Children benefit greatly from authentic relationships with us. They learn about their self-identity from us, and how to be critical-thinking, responsible citizens of the world. When we are humane to them, they learn to be humane to others. When we allow them to explore their emotions safely, they trust us more, and when they trust us, they open themselves up to learn more and more from us—and also to share some of their innermost feelings with us.

About This Book

Over the years, many of you have asked me for advice about what to do with those children who need our attention. My response to you is this book. We all have needed attention in some form or another when we were children, and if we are honest with ourselves, we probably still crave it even as adults. So, let's get to work. It is a complex subject indeed, because I imagine everyone has a different idea about what constitutes attention and how and why we need it. In chapters 1 and 2, the topic at large is discussed, including anecdotes from my personal life as well as stories about children I have known or observed. I try to provide a general sense of what we are talking about. Why do young children need attention? Why is giving it to them important?

As I was sitting in a coffee shop editing these pages, a father was sitting at a nearby table with his two children. His daughter was about five or six years old, and the son around two. After a while, it became clear to me that the father was teaching his girl how to play chess. As they each played their moves, the father gently discussed why and how his daughter was choosing to move her chess pieces where she did. They were having an interesting, intellectual chess discussion between the two of them—he was most respectful of his daughter's capabilities and ideas. Soon, his son, the toddler, became agitated, calling out, falling off his seat, and begging to go home in a loud, whiny voice. Other adults in the coffee shop were becoming antsy, shifting in their seats and looking critically at the family, disrupting their quiet morning of reading, looking at computer screens, or listening to music through headphones.

Soon the father picked up his son and held him tenderly in his lap, talking to him about this and that as he continued playing chess with his daughter. When it was time for them to leave, I went over to the father and told him I was writing a book about children needing attention. He gave me an exhausted smile. He said, "You mean, all of them? And all kinds of attention?" I returned the smile and replied that I thought he was kind, respectful, and caring in his interactions with his children, and that I couldn't help noticing their interactions since I happened to be in the middle of writing about children needing attention. He sighed and thanked me profusely. I thought to myself, "Parents need to hear when things are going right!"

In chapter 3, I discuss self-regulation and self-control, specifically with regard to helping children develop skills about how to negotiate attention with significant adults in their lives. We can support them through this negotiation, or we can leave them alone to work it out by themselves. Once again, I bring us back to how we connect with how we were taught to self-regulate as children and how that affects the way we teach children to self-soothe.

"When Teachers Face Themselves" is the name of chapter 4. First, I share my story and show how I understand things about myself in relation to how I feel about how I sought out attention. Then I provide some ideas for your own self-reflection. This is a chapter that could also be called "Awareness Is Key!" When I am more aware about why I do what I do, I am able to be more responsible, responsive, and intentional in my work with young children. As Carol Garboden Murray says, "We do not take care of human beings the same way we take care of a house or a lawn" (Murray 2017). Unintentional mistakes we make cutting the lawn or cleaning our house are not as critical as unintentional interactions that hurt a child emotionally. Taking care of children is an awesome responsibility, and to become professional, we need to be more and more aware and intentional with our interactions and behaviors. I revisit this when I write more about self-reflection in chapter 6.

Chapter 5 could be titled my advice chapter. I could also call it, "What Works for Me Does Not Always Work for You!" Expanding on the notion that every child is unique, I discuss ways of thinking about how we can interact with children by creating authentic relationships in everything we do, including designing the physical environment and doling out praise for the many "good jobs" that children do in the classroom. Strategies for attention getting, receiving, and withholding are shared.

The book concludes with a chapter about developing compassion and empathy skills to enhance your ability to connect with all the children in your classroom. But, also, you learn how to be compassionate with yourself because of the hard work you do day in and day out as you care for and educate young children. I revisit the idea that we become professional when we are intentional with our behaviors and interactions. To that end, self-reflection and how we change our worldview become an important part of the discussion.

Everyone, including adults, needs attention, validation, and acknowledgment. After all, we learn about who we are and develop our self-identity by and from the reactions and interactions with people outside of ourselves—family members, teachers, and society at large (Mead 1967). We need one another for affirmation. We cannot go it alone. As Bruce Perry reminds us in the final chapter of *The Boy Who Was Raised as a Dog,* "The truth is, you cannot love yourself unless you have been loved and are loved. The capacity to love cannot be built in isolation" (Perry and Szalavitz 2006, 234).

So, dear reader, I invite you to dive in with me on this oftentimes very personal journey that I have chosen to share with you. Along the way, you may find out things about yourself that will be a revelation of joy and gratitude. On the other hand, you could also dredge up feelings from the past that are uncomfortable, or even painful. Either way, you will get to know yourself better and, most importantly, be available and accessible to young children with authentic emotions to help them discover theirs. We can't lose if we do it for the sake of children.

Chapter 1

May I Have Your Attention Please?

What I've come to understand is that the most important work I do to see a child in positive ways is within me. I must continually work to transform my own view of children's behaviors, see their points of view, and strive to uncover how what I am seeing reveals the children's deep desire, eagerness, and capacity for relationships. There is no more important or rewarding work than this. —Deb Curtis (2017)

DRIVING DOWN THE ROAD THE OTHER DAY, reflecting on this or that personal situation happening in my life, I suddenly experienced a rush of emotion that tapped into an old feeling from childhood. It brought tears to overflowing and surprised me so much that I exclaimed out loud alone in the car, "Please don't hurt me. I want you to love me." I realized then how much I had longed for my mother to love me even when she disapproved of my behavior. Perhaps I needed her support especially because I was struggling to find my own identity, even if it meant pushing against her will. These thoughts sprung up mainly because I had been thinking about mothering in the broadest sense, especially since a few days before when I witnessed a young mother being harsh with her young child at a coffee shop where I had gone to write.

One of the core challenges in parenting or teaching young children is creating boundaries for them without repressing their authentic emotional selves. *Please don't hurt them—they want us to love them.* That's the dance, the constant negotiation. We want our children to be safe and successful, and we act like we know the way to get them there. We have learned from our parents and our own mistakes. We have learned what to fear and what not to care about in order to survive and become successful ourselves. We have developed a perspective and worldview about how children should behave and what constitutes success in general. We pour our fears, biases, and survival skills all over our smallest children and try to formulate little people in our own image. We do all of this with good intentions and love—whatever that is. Because what do we know about love other than the way we have been loved?

Are we loving in the same way we were loved, or are we trying not to do what was done to us? Whatever all that amounts to, do we really know who our children are? What they aspire to? What they fear or long for? So much of what they do is either to please or push against us, depending on their developmental age. At the core of a young child must be a feeling that they cannot express: *"Please don't hurt me. I want you to love me."* Young children need our love to survive, but they also want us to love them for who they are, for their unique constellation of characteristics and personality.

Can we love them fat or thin, shiny or sad, angry and grumpy, joyous and loudly enthusiastic? Can we rejoice in their independent thinking, sexuality, and smarts, support their confusion and insecurities, and not take it personally? As they find out who they are, what they need or desire, and how to express themselves emotionally, can we be there for them with full attention, love, and support for that exploration?

The process is complex to be sure, for how much do we really know ourselves? Are we aware of how our own early childhood affected our worldview, or are those memories already repressed somewhere deep in our psyche? What do we do to get in touch with those feelings, and if we recognize them, how much do we allow ourselves to face them? How do we allow our children to follow their hearts all the while loving them for it, even when they are so different from who we are?

Developing a Compassionate Worldview

Whenever we read a nonfiction book about education or child development, we approach it with a worldview all our own, one that we have developed along the way through our own early childhood experiences, with knowledge about how children behave and learn, and from what we are familiar with in practice. Herbert Kohl describes his worldview as "discovering what is right about [children], and then [being] ingenious in discovering what works for them. . . . [His] philosophy of education . . . is based on a strength model of children, not a deficiency model" (2009, xxii).

So, here is some point of counsel for the reader. For this book, it may be helpful for you to reach for a compassionate worldview—an understanding that children are *whole*, complex human beings influenced by genetics as well as their socioemotional and cultural environment. They are not simply a sum of behaviors. So, if you are a proponent of manipulating, modifying, and controlling children's behaviors with punishments and rewards, you may experience discomfort with some of the opinions, ideas, and beliefs in this book. On the other hand, perhaps I can change your mind, present you with a different option to think about other than the way you perceive things at this moment in your life. After all, I am an educator by profession, and I believe that one of my main goals is to give you another option to think about—a provocation, if you will, so that you may think about things a little differently than before.

I have been in the field of early childhood education for over forty years in one form or another: as a student, preschool/kindergarten teacher, director of a child care center, professor of early childhood education, teacher educator, supervisor of student teachers, consultant, accreditation validator, adviser, presenter, author, and mother. I have seen a lot! I have seen teachers who listen, connect, and relate to children with compassion and patience. At other times, however, I have observed teachers using strategies like denying food to children, grabbing them by the arm, and pushing them harshly into a chair, humiliating or shaming them in order to manipulate their behaviors over and over again, and my heart has ached to the point of weeping.

Many of these same teachers have good intentions, and some are only doing what they learned or what was done to them when they were young. Some have described a worldview that prepares children for hard knocks in a harsh, cruel world "out there." Indeed, when questioned, some of these teachers suggested to me that they were doing it for "the children's own good." And yet I understand more and more that we treat others the way we were treated. So, if we treat others harshly, with shaming and contempt or physical aggression, it is extremely likely that they will go on to do the same with others. Children are not simply a bundle of behaviors that we can control with stickers or time-outs. They are complex human beings constantly constructing knowledge, with feelings, experiences, and opinions. They deserve better. They deserve complex interactions unique to each one of them. At the very least, they deserve our full attention as we get to know them.

I believe that a book about children's need for attention is an important addition to the literature for early childhood educators. I fully realize that in the early childhood education world, there may be some resistance to what I propose from certain behaviorists—parents and teachers alike—pushing for self-regulation by using punishments and rewards. My view is that children need our full-on authentic attention. They need us to see them as whole human beings, not just the sum of their behaviors. They need us to listen to them, to validate their feelings, and to take them seriously for who they are and the people they will grow into.

I believe this first and foremost from personal experience. I did not receive the kind of attention that I believe children deserve. I was not listened to with respect, and my feelings were deemed unwarranted and destructive, so much so that to this day I have difficulty trusting the validity of my emotions. I was almost never taken seriously during my childhood. I know how wounded children can become if they don't receive the type of attention they need. I believe my emotional survival was dependent mostly on the kindness of strangers. As an older adult, I have come to understand the reasons behind how I was treated, and while I imagine and hope that there were no conscious intentions to hurt me, I was, in fact, hurt—emotionally wounded—and have had to work hard throughout my life to unlearn the emotional life script I was taught, and to relearn how to make choices that are not self-destructive.

Children Deserve Our Attention

I advocate, therefore, for the type of relationships for children with significant adults in their lives that will give them the attention they deserve for their emotional development and mental health: unwavering support for their needs, opinions, and self-expression in general and commitment to defending them and making a stand for their emotional integrity and self-worth. Anything short of that is too little for young children in our care.

Children need to feel worthwhile. They don't just need our praise. Rather, they need to feel that their opinions and achievements are acknowledged and supported by the types of discussions we have with them about their work and play and about the way they think or feel about things that are important to them. This is how we take them seriously. It is not by trivializing them by saying they are pretty or cute or by patting them on the head with an empty comment like "Good job!" which really tells them nothing of value about what they have done or said. Instead, we take them seriously by extending the discussion and listening—really listening to what they have to say—and by asking them open-ended questions that expand their thinking (Dombro, Jablon, and Stetson 2011).

We are children's guardians and guides. We are their mentors and protectors. If we humiliate or hurt them, they have nowhere to turn. They become helpless and powerless unless we empower them with kindness and compassion. There is no one fix or one size that fits everyone, because each child is unique genetically, psychologically, and socioculturally. Each child has completely different life experiences one from the other, as well as from me. I must develop empathy and compassion to work with children, or I should not be anywhere near them!

I invite you to be willing to reflect on your own childhood experiences about receiving or being denied the attention you craved and deserved, even though this may be painful at times. Everyone needs attention—especially young children. It makes us feel valued and recognized. Children need our attention to validate who they are and what they think and feel.

From our earliest years, we seek out adult attention, and depending on how we do not or do receive it, or the manner in which we receive it, we will learn whether we are worthy of it—whether to be ashamed or not that we want it. Some of us will crave attention for the rest of our lives but not know how to ask for it, or will have great difficulty ever feeling deserving of it.

Defining Attention

Attention means different things to different people and comes in many forms: it can be any form of receiving acknowledgment, validation, or recognition, of being noticed, heard, or seen. It can involve getting gifts, rewards, or awards. It may be being sought out, teased, tickled, shouted at, called out on the carpet, or punished. It can include being considered sexually attractive, smart, or talented—the list is endless. I am sure you can add your own understanding of what attention means for you.

As a child, I longed to be noticed. I wanted to be singled out and to become a priority for the adults in my life. I wanted people to stand up for me. I wanted to belong, feel wanted, and be yearned for. I wanted to be someone's priority. When I shared my wisdom or smarts, I wanted to be taken seriously. I wanted to be liked and loved for my singing, intelligence, sexuality, knowledge, and good deeds. I wanted people to want me around. But it took me many years—up until I was in my sixties—to acknowledge that I, like everyone else, wanted attention. And that I, like everyone else, deserved it.

The Many Forms of Attention

Attention comes in many forms. It is not just noticing that you exist. It is noticing who you are in all your uniqueness. I remember years ago when I defended my doctoral dissertation. I enjoyed those couple of hours more than anything I can remember. It was not only about the doctoral committee members approving of or liking my work. It was about people relating in depth to the *meaning* of my work with curiosity and open-ended questions that stimulated me to explore my topic further. Their relating to me in that manner gave me a deep and lasting feeling of accomplishment and self-worth.

Many months ago, I was having lunch with my son in Manhattan. He is in his forties—an accomplished jazz pianist with a graduate degree in family therapy. He asked me what I was working on, and I described to him my concern about children's need for attention and how challenging it can be for teachers. As we chatted back and forth, he reminded me that giving or withholding attention is complex. It is more than just noticing someone, he stated passionately. It is about interactions. It has to do with relationship. I was moved by how he tenderly shared with me the ways in which he sought my attention when he was a young child. I am constantly grateful for my son, because ever since he was born, I have learned so much from him. And here, too, he reminded me that attention is about interactions and our behaviors toward one another—it has everything to do with how we relate to one another.

What Happens When We Ignore Those Who Need Our Attention?

I do not know how many times I have heard a teacher or parent say, "Oh, she/he is just doing it for attention." And then they follow up with, "so just ignore her/him." I am sure that if I have not actually used that expression myself, I have certainly thought it—about others, as well as about myself, and not in a positive way. From the very earliest years, adults frequently silence and trivialize children. We scold them for wanting our attention and shush them, defining *good* children as silent, obedient, or self-regulating—those who do not take up too much of our time, energy, or *attention*. In some form or another, we have all been taught that "children should be seen and not heard." In short, we shame children and make them feel guilty for wanting our attention in the first place.

Reaching into the recesses of my memory, I learn about how I came to be me. As an older adult, I find myself repeating over and over again what I did for attention as a young child. Back then my mother was emotionally unavailable for me. During those years, I believe that she did not feel safe emotionally and, therefore, could not make space for me. Even as I understand how I developed this way, I find it an extraordinary challenge to alter my behavior and feelings associated with it. For example, when I was a child, one of the ways I tried to get attention was by serving others (namely, my mother or father) while putting my needs last. And then, if I was noticed for my "goodness," I felt worthwhile. I have dragged that baggage around with me right up to the present day. The trouble with this method is that I feel I have to serve and sacrifice for a long time before I am noticed for my goodness. By then, I am exhausted, frustrated, and resentful, and after briefly feeling worthwhile, I lash out—much to the shock of everyone around me. Then I feel ashamed and guilty for my outburst and immediately return to serving and sacrificing. This full cycle of attention-getting behavior might have helped me survive as a child but is quite unproductive and even destructive for me now.

I think about blogging, Twitter, and Facebook. Don't we just love the attention? Posting our thoughts, photographs, and birthday dates just so that others out there in cyberspace will see, hear, and respond to us? Indeed, through social media, we receive constant and immediate gratification, validation, and acknowledgment, in short—attention! I often find myself thinking or even saying out loud to myself, "Am I just doing this [whatever it is] for attention?" I feel shame when I seek it and constantly hear people judging others for being an "attention-getter."

Where and why do teachers perceive children's need for attention as something negative—something that gets in the way of their learning? I am reminded of a sensitive and vulnerable kindergartner one morning during his third morning meeting, when he was required to sit still and follow the teacher-directed assignments. Clearly, he wanted to share his point of view, became excited and passionate about the topic being discussed, and wanted to be noticed—all at the same time. After three times being told to sit still and be quiet, he was sent away to sit alone at a table while the rest of his classmates participated in the story and discussion. He even tried raising his hand out there in punished isolation—to no avail.

He was being taught self-regulation, and any feelings of loneliness or anxiety about being excluded—well, he would have to deal with them alone. It was no wonder that later, once he had completed the assigned task of cutting and pasting, he would not make any extra effort to color in the pictures he had glued on the teacher's precut paper. His anger was palpable, although I could tell he was swallowing it down into his emotional memory. I thought about how one day all those repressed and swallowed angry feelings would probably have to bubble up and out somewhere. And would he be alone with those feelings? Would someone be around at the time to support him through the veritable storm he would rage? Or would he just become chronically ill, allowing those feelings to eat him from within?

Haven't We Always Longed for Attention?

Don't we all want attention? Don't we all want to have our feelings, ideas, and self-expression validated, acknowledged, supported, or related to in some way? How do we really know what is the right amount of attention a person needs? Can we imagine what it feels like as an older, younger, or middle sibling to have to share attention? Can a person want too much attention? Brain development research shows us that to feel attached and worthwhile, children need our love, touch, and full-on attention to survive. They could die without it—indeed, some do. Children must know what we think about them. They need our validation and acknowledgment for their emotional survival. And when they do not receive it, they compensate in all kinds of ways: repressing their needs and wants, shouting and becoming aggressive or violent, going underground and harboring resentment alone, or seeking it from anyone who will give it to them. Children feel invisible when they are unnoticed. I know I did!

Once, when I was presenting at a national conference in Orlando, I asked the participants to think about ways in which they sought attention when they were children. There was a pause, and just when I thought that no one would be forthcoming with an answer, a woman in her forties called out in the distance, "I got attention by being perfect." When I looked in her direction, I noticed that she was emotional. I repeated, "You had to be perfect." She nodded her head. I asked gently, "Does saying this out loud make you emotional?" She nodded again, and tears filled her eyes. Later, when I recounted this story to another early childhood colleague, she said, "I wonder how many people who became teachers were children who got attention by being perfect." I thought to myself, "I wonder. . . ."

I had a lousy childhood. In fact, I would say I did not have a childhood at all, because my days were fraught with worrying about how my mother was feeling, and when I played, I played alone, silently in my room. To this day, I still have a hard time "playing." Once, the staff of the child care center where I was director took me on an outing to Disneyland when we were at a conference in Los Angeles. I was like a small child—*oohing* and *aahing*, laughing out loud at the rides, and walking around in wonder. They were surprised, because I did not allow Disney characters to decorate the walls of our child care center—only real pictures of children and their families, or prints of artwork from the local art gallery. But I felt like a child being taken out to play, and I soaked up every moment.

As a child, I was a scapegoat for my mother's anxieties, fears, and rage. She gave birth to me at an inconvenient time for her during a brief second marriage with a man she disliked, all the while having an affair with my future stepfather through the four or five dismally volatile years she lived with my father. Once she married my stepfather, she spent the rest of their married life in and out of rage at him or in fear of abandonment by him. My being a part of that mix just complicated everything even more. And she let me know it, warning me not to make too much noise or eat too much food lest my stepfather would notice. When they had my younger brother, I was eight years old, and I must have felt that whatever was left of my already tenuous birthright vanished immediately and forever. I remember my childhood as a dark and fearful time, all the while doing everything I could to go unnoticed. Now and then when I attempted to make a stand for myself even as a young child, some of the ways I sought attention were through outbursts, migraines, or sickness. Alas, it was in vain, for my mother's attention came at me in the form of terrifying wrath—shaming me into believing I was a destructive and hateful being.

Knowing what I know now about early childhood development, care, and education, I am aware that abused children believe that they deserve punishment from their parents because they feel they are at fault. Therefore, I understand that it was impossible for me not to believe that at my core I was a worthless and unwanted being. Looking back as a woman with silvery hair in her late sixties, an accomplished early childhood professional, author, and teacher, I realize that somehow through all the abuse I managed to hold on to to a hope that I might one day deserve better. As a survivor, I developed resilience through searching for support through the kindness of strangers. Growing up, I discovered ways to belong by joining organizations and groups whose ideology included compassion for the human condition and a belief that we are all in this together. Each time I tried to love or help others feel included, I retained pieces of the feelings for me. Sitting around hating and whining never became my shtick. Lately, as I continue to heal, I seek out those who are nonjudgmental and able to accept me as I am. Of course, I still struggle with self-acceptance and self-compassion. And I realize that at some level I probably always will.

The Complexity of Human Emotion

> There is no safe place emotionally or physically in the education and development of teachers for confronting uncomfortable feelings they might have. . . . It is not possible for

> teachers to refer children to their colleagues [like counselors do] or seek counseling supervision in the context of education. Teachers just have to get on with it one way or another. As a result, young children are the recipients of many of our harmful, unconscious behaviors.
>
> —Tamar Jacobson (2003)

We all were children once and, as adults, probably carry within us different ways of dealing with stifling our desire for attention. Half the battle to understanding this basic need for attention is to acknowledge it as being important in the first place, at least giving ourselves permission for wanting it. When we remember what we did as children to be noticed and to feel important to significant adults in our lives, we can better understand and negotiate children's need for attention.

For example, awhile ago when I was presenting a workshop on this topic, I asked the participants to reflect on their own childhood and specifically about how they sought attention from their parents. One of the women shared that she sought attention by taking toys away from her younger sister. As we discussed the incidents further, she revealed that she was anxious and jealous of her younger sister and that in fact she had taken the toys because she was hurting. I described to her an ideal scenario where her parents, instead of admonishing her about taking away the toy, might have held her in their arms and told her how much they loved her and understood her pain about her younger sister. I described this alternate version of her parents by saying something like, "We don't expect you to love your sister until you are ready. We love her and you, and one day we are sure you will love your sister too—when you are more used to her being in our lives. We can't allow you to take away her toys because that hurts her, but we love you nevertheless and understand why you are doing this." The woman in the audience who had shared her situation began to weep. She said she realized that she always thought she sought out negative attention, when, in fact, she just needed to have her feelings validated.

"Attention getting" is a complex issue in our work with young children. I wonder how we deal with children's need for attention when we had to develop all kinds of unique ways of seeking it ourselves. What makes us uncomfortable about desiring attention? Does it make us feel guilty or ashamed for even wanting it in the first place? One time I was presenting a workshop for early childhood educators in Nova Scotia. I asked the participants whether they felt uncomfortable having the focus on them. The majority of the audience raised their hands. When I asked who liked receiving attention, a woman raised her hand cautiously to say that she enjoyed having the focus on her. She was one of two or three who raised their hands gingerly in an audience of two hundred people.

How might feelings of shame or guilt influence our giving or withholding attention from children? Do we see it as children needing or deserving our attention, or *demanding* it? Do teachers prefer the "good, obedient, self-regulating" child? For another example, on a flight from Philadelphia to Orlando last year, I heard a young mother apologize to the women seated next to her on the plane for the noise her sixteen-month-old child *might* make, even before her daughter had opened her mouth.

One summer morning while reading a column in the *New York Times* (Wayne 2014), I glanced at the terms *ego sustenance* and *social media* in the same sentence. I thought to myself, there we go again—criticizing people for using social media to boost their egos. I know I do. And I know why. I love the attention. Having received so little of it as a child, this is one of the ways to fill up the hole in my soul that was created way back when. I feel supported and comforted when people notice my status updates or shares of one kind or another. So, rather than moaning and groaning about everyone needing "ego sustenance," let's turn our attention to early childhood care and education and think about how little acknowledgment we give to our youngest children. Indeed, I observe infant rooms all over the country and see over and over again that from the day children learn to vocalize sounds, they are being shushed and silenced.

I remember a recent breakfast in our local bakery when an older infant in a high chair at a table nearby was intentionally knocking his bottle on the table. From the serious, diligent look of pleasure on his face, I could tell he was experimenting with the sound of it. After a number of *tap-taps* of the bottle, it was whisked—nay, forcibly grabbed—from his hands, and an irritated-looking mother slammed it down on the table next to her far away from his reach. He sat staring straight ahead, startled and confused for a long moment. Then he looked toward me. I smiled at him, and he smiled back, a small sigh escaping from his lips. I imagined that as they were in an adult establishment—a bakery for breakfast—maybe the mother was worried he was making too much noise for the people around them. And yet I wonder: Young children's squeals and squeaks, tap-tapping of bottles and toys could, on the other hand, delight us—like music to our ears. For what could be more amazing than a young child discovering his voice or learning a new skill?

Being more aware of our own emotional development will help us give loads of loving attention to all those young children out there—starting from the day they are born. We will be able to relate more objectively to what they say and do and help them feel worthwhile through authentic relationships. What a concept!

Chapter 2

Why Everyone Needs Attention

Today's moment that absolutely melted my heart . . . one of the younger toddlers has been saying "hey" to get my attention, especially in recent weeks. This afternoon, instead of saying "hey," she called me "eeen," which might be one of the sweetest variations in my name I've ever heard. And she was so proud when she said it. She used it several times just this afternoon when starting an interaction with me, and my heart just about melted and exploded with joy at the same time. This particular child and I have had a good relationship all year, but in recent months and weeks our attachment has definitely flourished and deepened. It's moments like this that just remind me of how lucky and grateful I am to work in a field and in a job that fits me so well. I love that there are literally moments of joy scattered throughout every single day when working with young children. —*Colleen Walling, lead teacher (2017)*

A FEW YEARS AGO, I brought home a pair of kittens. They were four months old. The last of a litter of six, four of which had been adopted before I found these two in a large cage at the pet store. In retrospect, I probably acquired them too soon after my beloved cat Ada's death that same year. I had not even begun to grieve her, and yet the house felt so lonely without her that one morning I found myself on the way to the pet store. After looking at the choices of paired kittens in different cages, I settled on Oscar and Mimi. Little gray Oscar seemed fragile and vulnerable, and I loved him instantly. His sister, Mimi, was strong and healthy—lithe and sharp-eyed. My love for her would come later. As I drove away from the pet store, I noticed that Oscar's eye was becoming milky, but that did not deter me. I decided that with a few eye drops and a lot of love, he would be cured quickly. I had also observed that he was especially quiet and inactive for a kitten that young, but still I soldiered on.

As it turned out, Oscar was very ill with feline infectious peritonitis (FIP), and within a few months would die. He became weaker, blinder, unstable on his legs, and unable to run, climb, and play with his sister. Mimi, on the other hand, was becoming larger, stronger, and more robust. She had a healthy appetite and would eat almost all of Oscar's food, especially since he would leave his bowl after one or two bites. For the few months of Oscar's life, I hovered anxiously by their food bowls, trying to coax him to eat more while keeping Mimi from gobbling up what he was unable to digest. It was a constant battle, and watching little Oscar become weaker and more ailing was excruciating. I tried to hold on to his life, all the while blaming myself for not being able to help him more.

During this time, I started to notice how I would stare at Mimi when she hid from Oscar and then charged out and pounced on him in play, took food from his bowl, and prevented him from sitting on any chair in the living room. Finally, I found myself glaring at her even when she simply walked into a room. Sometimes I whispered under my breath about her to myself, "The beast," or "That greedy beast." I began to dislike myself around her, feeling guilty and ashamed for unkind thoughts toward her. One day, as Mimi tussled with Oscar on the carpet in my study, I became disturbingly aware that I was glaring at her with hatred. The feeling came from somewhere deep inside me. I held still, trying to understand what was happening to me, when suddenly I understood to the core of my being that when I was a young child, my mother had glared at me like that. Indeed, I knew that *look* intimately. I had seen and felt it like a knife that cut into and through me. At first I felt nauseous, as if I was about to throw up, and then I started to weep. Tears poured down my cheeks in torrents as I sobbed for what seemed like forever. I experienced pain in my chest and in my joints and burning sensations in my stomach. My head started to throb. I was in agony remembering those looks from my mother—terrifying and rejecting. Her anger and what felt like hatred of me penetrated to the core, heart and soul.

When I was done crying and the pain began to dissipate, I left my chair and sat limp and exhausted on the rug close to the two kittens. I picked Mimi up in my arms and buried my head in her soft fur, shedding just one or two more leftover tears. I whispered into her ears, "I am so sorry, Mimi. I am so, so sorry." She lay quietly purring, as I realized I wasn't really apologizing to the kitten but to little Tamarika (my father's nickname for me) from all those years ago, that young-me-child, who had never heard that apology until that moment. I felt released, relieved, and peaceful.

From that moment, I have not only looked at Mimi differently—like a typical kitten who needs to play, eat, grow, and develop—I have also grown to love her. I was able to comfort her when she searched and pined for her brother days and weeks after he died, and for the following four months, I loved her with every fiber of my being. I thought I was healing her from my hateful glares, but, in fact, all the while I was healing myself. From then on, I experienced a shift in my own psychological development and awareness. Indeed, I started to allow myself to really experience my early childhood pain—so necessary for shedding ancient shame and fear in my present life and relationships. Recently, when we acquired a new kitten, who coincidentally was also named Oscar, I was happy to see Mimi gently and kindly take him under her wing in a playful yet nurturing way.

More importantly, though, once again I had reinforced and reconfirmed my theory that our own early emotional memory of punishment affects our feelings and interactions with children with regard to discipline. For while I understand cats and children are very different, I realized that if I had not allowed myself to confront the agony of remembering fear and rejection from my own mother's glare, I might not have prevented myself from hating and even perhaps abusing a small, innocent kitten.

Children Seeking Attention (Wanting Relationship)

During one of my latest breakout sessions at a conference, the participants discussed how they associated children needing attention with mostly negative behaviors. They described the negative ways in which they sought attention as children, like tattling, being sickly, making weird faces, jumping in front of the camera, and making more work for their mother. At a certain moment during the presentation, I asked, "What if instead of saying (or thinking), 'She is just doing it for attention . . . ignore her,' we said (or thought) instead, 'She is just doing it for relationship.'" After I said that, there was silence in the room. I stood before the participants and waited, watching for their reaction. Attendees stared back at me for almost a minute. Now it seemed that we could discuss children's need for attention differently.

When we replace *wanting attention,* with its negative connotation, with *wanting relationship,* we start thinking of different ways we can respond. For example, ignoring the child is no longer an option—in relationships we usually don't ignore a person crying out for us. Instead, we are present: listening, observing, and waiting patiently. I wondered why children's needing or wanting attention has become such a negative idea in the first place. Why do people say that it is best to ignore someone who needs our attention? Where do these ideas, thoughts, and feelings come from? Did we learn this early on as children, as our parents or teachers could not provide us with the attention we needed, thus making us understand that it was bad, or even shameful, to want it in the first place? Is it culturally influenced in the sense that different cultures may address children's need for attention as something positive? Is it gender influenced in that boys and girls may need or receive attention differently? How does all of this tie into our expectations of children? For example, some people derive pleasure from children being active, messy, and noisy and asking lots of questions. Others feel put upon—they describe children as making too much noise and show disdain when they talk too much or too loudly.

According to Emily Plank (2016), Americans in particular have a misguided worldview about children needing attention. Americans come from a culture that has a "get what you deserve" bias, which makes people believe that children are manipulating us and that we are in danger of being controlled by those little "con artists" if we give in to them by giving them attention. She goes on to warn us that this is a misunderstanding of the culture of childhood:

> Attention is a difficult hurdle for adults. We are so deeply enmeshed in the narrative that "you get what you pay for" that extending attention to a child as a fundamental right of her humanity, despite her behavior, seems impossible. . . . Attention is not a tool of manipulation. Attention is a piece of the equation whereby children know they belong to the community around them. (Plank 2016, 163)

Children need our attention not only to survive as infants but also, and just as importantly, to discover who they are—to develop a sense of identity and self-worth—and not only to become conscious and more aware of themselves but to develop self-consciousness. In 1934 the famous social philosopher George Herbert Mead wrote about how we develop a sense of self because of our experiences with others, or, more specifically, as a result of others' attitudes and interactions toward us:

> The individual experiences himself as such . . . from the particular standpoints of other individual members of the same social group. . . . For he enters his own experience as a self or individual . . . and he becomes an object to himself [becoming self-conscious] only by taking the attitudes of other individuals toward himself within a social environment or context of experience and behavior in which both he and they are involved. (Mead 1967, 138)

Donald Winnicott (1987), a British psychoanalyst, suggested that in fact there is no such thing as "independence," because an individual cannot really survive without acknowledging her place in society. He stated that if a person was so withdrawn from society that she felt "independent and invulnerable," she was sure to have mental health problems. We learn about who we are and how to feel about ourselves through interactions with others.

One night I was at dinner with friends, who asked me how the writing of this book was coming along. The husband of my friend, who is a psychiatrist, asked me what the book was about. Trying to be brief and to move on to other subjects, like their delicious dinner, I said, "It's a book for teachers about children needing attention." "Don't they know that already?" he exclaimed. He went on animatedly, "If they don't, why are they working with children?" I thought about what he said, and early the next day pulled a book off my shelf that described the research about social-emotional learning and academic success (Zins et al. 2004). As I expected, the authors concluded that "caring relations between teachers and students foster a desire to learn and a connection to school." How we interact and behave with children has an effect on their feelings of self-worth. How we attend to children matters. *Caring relations* matter. So, I would answer my friend, "Yes, I think that teachers know that already. The research tells us so." But as I will discuss further, not only what we *know* to be good early childhood practice but also what we *feel* about our own early childhood experiences affect our interactions.

Connecting the Personal with the Professional

As I recount my own story about my childhood and how my relationships with significant adults in my life affected how I became who I am today, I find that the subject is way too personal for me to talk about objectively. I make connections between my story and how I view what is important about relationships with our youngest children. For example, when I see children ignored or neglected emotionally, I feel it viscerally. My eyes begin to smart, I sense a tightening in my throat, chest, and stomach, and I want to cry out. Sometimes tears start to well up and run down my cheeks. That is when I realize that my feelings are not only a reaction about the child's experience but also related to an emotional memory about my own childhood.

To survive my childhood, I learned to stifle all feelings I had when I was neglected or ignored emotionally. That doesn't mean the feelings weren't there all along. Lately, now that I am well into my sixties and no longer fear my mother, I am more able to experience the feelings I stifled so long ago. To understand my feelings and concerns about children's need for attention, I make a connection with my own childhood so that I can make decisions based on professional knowledge and not *only* on personal life experience. As I reflect on my life, I realize that people who have positively affected my self-worth listened to me, encouraged and supported me, and showed me affection. These were all ways of giving me attention. They remembered things I had told them, and they believed what I said.

As I was growing up, I developed a daydream with a recurring theme. I would think about it and fantasize whenever I was alone, riding to school on my bicycle, walking in the yard among the plants and ferns, or playing with my dolls alone in my bedroom. The theme was that I would quietly do very good deeds—even heroic ones—and then one day I would be discovered. Sometimes it was a romantic discovery by a charming man, who could not help but notice how kind and sweet I was—a sort of Cinderella story. Other times, I was discovered for my smarts or courage as a social justice activist. Indeed, by the age of sixteen, I was writing down stories using my new little typewriter my mother had given me for my birthday. One of the stories was called, "Bombs Won't Stop Me," in which a young girl parachuted into Germany during the Second World War and saved hundreds of Jews from the gas chambers.

During the last weeks of my mother's life as I sat quietly by her bedside while she slept, I stroked her hair and held her hand. I played her a piece of cello music that I thought would soothe her, and I told her over and over again how much I loved her. When she died, I realized that I was waiting for her to notice me one last time and recognize me for quietly loving her and for my good deeds that would otherwise go unnoticed. The hardest part for me about her dying was that she never did discover me, recognize my smarts, or acknowledge my courage. In fact, all those fantasies I had as a child were really about my longing for my mother to notice me. I realized that I was waiting for it until the end of her life. Perhaps I could feel some relief now, because there would be no more walking into a room hoping to be recognized by her.

Even more profound for me recently is the realization that not only did I need attention, but I also longed for it and enjoyed it when I received it. However, as an adult, each time I received attention or awards—recognition for a good presentation or introductions about my expertise at conferences—even as I enjoyed the acknowledgment, I immediately felt sheepish or ashamed of receiving too much of it. I felt as if it was wrong to want it—and certainly bad to enjoy receiving it. These feelings have made me wonder: at what point do we make children stifle their need for attention, and how do we go about making them feel ashamed or guilty for enjoying receiving it? In addition, I wonder if attention is only about acknowledgment, or is it more profound because it is connected to how we relate to each other—how we listen and thus validate one another?

Recently, I had the good fortune to listen to a keynote speech at a conference by Toni Christie (2017), in which she reminded us about the concept of *filling the bucket*, from early childhood advocate Magda Gerber, meaning that full-on, quality attention fills the child up emotionally for an extended period of time, whereas scraps of attention leave the child with an ongoing hunger for more. Respect is key to relationships, Christie said, as she quoted Dr. Seuss, "A person's a person no matter how small." At the same conference, Peter Mangione (2017) reminded us that "we have a small window when young children are lovable and loved—and that is infancy." He stressed that children love relationship. They feel worthwhile and valued through relationship.

Caroline Knapp, in her book about *why women want*, and in her own understanding of how she became anorexic, describes the importance of being safe and recognized and the pain of unmet need for children whose mothers were not attuned or responsive to them:

> Being known. This, of course, is the goal, the agenda so carefully hidden it may be unknown even to the self. The anorexic starves to make manifest her hunger and vulnerability. The extremes announce, This is who I am, this is what I feel. In quadrophonic sound, they give voice to the most central human hunger, which is the desire to be recognized, to be known and loved because of and in spite of, who you are; to give voice to the sorrow that takes root when that hunger is unsatisfied. (Knapp 2003, 175)

We all need recognition, acknowledgment, validation, relationship, to be heard, to have a voice, to be included, to contribute, to have our love received, valued, and accepted, for someone to accept our feelings, and to have some emotional space for sharing feelings. So, again, I ask, why is children's need for attention still so associated with negative behaviors?

What Do Teachers Think about Children and Attention?

Over the course of more than a year, I have been presenting at conferences across the country and facilitating professional development workshops. I asked participants, predominantly teachers or teacher educators, to share their thoughts as well as their own memories and experiences about children needing attention and about receiving it or not when they were children. Out of all the people who answered questionnaires I distributed, 76 percent wrote about children needing attention to thrive. When asked to write some thoughts about children needing attention, they said things like the following:

- All children need attention for a secured attachment to feel good about themselves. They need adults to be the "cheerleaders" for them in their lives.
- I believe that children need attention in a unique way. Each child needs attention differently. Some seek it out while others don't. It is up to the adults in a child's life . . . to provide an appropriate amount of attention in order for the child to continue to develop in a healthy manner.
- When children need attention . . . they typically need nurturing, love, grace, and caring.
- Children feel loved and protected when someone respects and acknowledges who they are, their feelings.

- Children need equal amounts of love, dedication, and compassion. All of these make up the attention.
- Catching the "I did it!" That moment of accomplishment when the child is so proud and looking for acknowledgment. The child looks around for you (Did you see me? Did you see me?) and you look them right in the eye, "Yeah! You did it!"
- One thing I've realized about children and attention is that children require undivided attention, and they will get attention whether it be good or bad, because they can't differentiate between the two in the moment. Being present, calm, and open with children is very important to avoid the negative attention moments.

A few noted that if children do not receive attention, they may misbehave or resort to aggressive behaviors and may be willing to receive negative attention rather than none at all. When asked about their own memories about receiving or not receiving attention when they were children, half the participants described single incidents or memories, sometimes in minute detail, of positive experiences:

- When I was about eight, I had scraped my knee and had a Band-Aid on my knee. It was stuck, and my mom wanted to just rip it off. But I cried, "No, it will hurt." My dad sat on the edge of the bed and quietly told me stories of his life growing up while just gently taking it off.
- I was a young child and had just come home and was upset, so as I went upstairs to my room, I sat down on the stairs and was crying about being bullied at school. When my grandma crawled up the stairs [to me] it made me smile. I'm almost sixty years old, and I still remember it as clear as can be!
- I remember the times my grandpa would get up in the mornings to take me to school. A little girl had been abducted, and once he saw that on the news, he would drive me to the bus

stop, which was only at the top of the hill, not even a mile. But he made sure he saw me get on the bus. He did this every day!

- My grandmother . . . lived close to us, so I was always able to visit whenever I wanted. She would have me over for "sleepovers." She had twin beds in her room. I always slept in the bed closest to the bathroom. My grandmother would always tuck me in and then would go into the bathroom to wash her face for bedtime. I always waited to fall asleep until she finished. I always felt loved and important to her.

In the other half of the responses, some of the stories were not as positive and even included a few outpourings of heartbreaking childhood memories. Some described how they thought these negative experiences affected them to this day:

- I received attention by being a sickly child. I'm the youngest of five children—I got attention by tattling on my siblings.
- Attention as a young child (before elementary school) was negative. "Do not make more work for your mother." Attention meant I was making work for her (single parent—marriage disintegrating or divorced). Best thing was to be invisible. I did not want attention. Hard to learn that attention was not a bad/painful thing.
- I can remember trying to get my mom to play with me. She would just lie on the couch and sleep. I felt as if I didn't matter. I was not important to her. That still affects me today. I am thirty-five, and I still try to get her to pay attention to me.
- Getting attention from my mom always meant being in trouble, or having disappointed her, or not being respectful or quiet, or not reading her mind. So, all but one of my siblings just tried to stay out of her way.
- As a child, I received very little attention. Even though I was the youngest child, I was "pushed to the back burner."

My father was physically, mentally, and emotionally abusive. . . . I usually got the worst amount of physical abuse because I would use my body to protect [my two stepbrothers] since I was older. [This person wrote a long story about her life of abuse in her family. She described experiencing mental anguish and major anxiety as an adult.]

- My dear mom suffered from bipolar depression. She often had severe bouts of depression that lasted for months and was hospitalized. I was an invisible child, an only child to two German immigrants who survived World War II. . . . I grew up with a lot of neglect. But when my mother was well, I was the center of her universe. It was quite bittersweet.
- Growing up in an abusive household, in the midst of drug and alcohol abuse, was awful. My sister and I were left alone much of the time or we were outside a lot. We learned to read body language and nonverbal cues early because we didn't want the negative attention. Today, at forty-six, I have emotional scars that are very deep. We did not receive loving attention, so I don't feel worthy of it today, although I know better.
- My little brother has Downs. I remember being so frustrated with how he would pester me and start pulling my hair. I never understood why. My mother always tried to tell me that when I wasn't giving him attention he tried resorting to negative behaviors to earn my attention. This is something I could not grasp until I went to school to work with young children. I was never able to be there as he needed.

After sharing this story about her experience with her brother and the guilt she still feels about not being there for him when she was a child, this teacher shared thoughts she had in general about attention. She added, "So many adults don't realize they are the same as children. We crave and need attention and don't always know healthy ways to ask for it. We are all holding on to a childlike piece of ourselves."

I remembered two incidents of needing and wanting attention when I was thirteen. In the first, I recall being bullied by one of the popular girls in the class (suddenly, as I write this, I remember her name and what she looked like all these five decades later). She called me a few anti-Semitic names and then said I came from a "broken home." I went home feeling dismayed, confused, and afraid. I told my mother about the incident, not really knowing how to proceed when I returned to school the next day. I asked my mother, "What did K. mean about a broken home?" My mother began shouting, crying, and wailing. "How dare you say you are from a broken home!" she yelled and continued to shout. I tried to tell her I hadn't said that, K. had. Eventually I would have to ask a teacher at school what the expression "a broken home" meant. Mainly I realized that asking that question caused my mother too much pain. I felt guilty that I had upset her like that and returned to school the next day to face bullying K. alone. I also learned that questioning my mother about something controversial was dangerous.

The second incident involved the only time my mother ever attended a school event of mine. Again, it was when I was twelve or thirteen. I had joined the school choir, and for some reason that I cannot remember, my mother decided to come and watch me sing. I was extremely excited to see her in the audience. I dressed especially well for the occasion and sang with gusto. I watched for her anxiously all the while I sang. When it was over, I raced down to the hall to see her. She looked at me with a grimace and said, "Why did you put your hair up like that? You were the only one with your hair up. It looked terrible." I remember feeling as if someone had punched me in the stomach. I slunk out of the hall with her, feeling ugly and worthless, and again ashamed that I had disappointed her like that. These incidents taught me that seeking attention was hurtful for my mother, and unpleasant and even dangerous for me.

The type of attention that involves relating to a child is very important. Attention is about authentic relationships and being related to. Being noticed and heard. How does a teacher or parent notice a child and still continue to relate to others? Everywhere I go people share memories of caring teachers who noticed them—who knew their names, said something encouraging to them, smiled at them. Infants search for their parents' eyes and smile at them when they are related to. They need attention as much as the milk they are given. They reach out their hands to be touched, and they grasp our fingers in return. It is all about relationships.

The Dangers of Trivializing Children

Relationships are at the heart of all learning. Children are interested in subjects when teachers communicate and discuss their ideas with them, listen to them, and take them seriously. Unfortunately, many adults trivialize children by laughing at them (even kindly) and calling them cute or pretty. Children are sharing their thoughts and ideas, and however absurd they seem to adults, children are serious about them. They need the opportunity to share what they are thinking and feeling so that they can understand who they are and what they believe and know. Even if it is a story about an imaginary tiger under her bed, the child needs to be able to tell her story to someone who listens and takes her seriously.

To that end, we need to learn empathy and compassion when we work with children because it is disrespectful to trivialize a child. Ignoring is hurtful and humiliating—disrespectful and cruel. Mocking, sarcasm, ostracizing, and teasing are too. The time-out is a form of ignoring someone—putting him aside, alone, to sort out what happened to or for him. These things can literally harm children emotionally for life! If we can't spend a lot of time with each child in our care, we have to devise a plan for how to do it at least some of the time with each one throughout the day. Sometimes we need to just be present with someone. We don't always have to fix or solve a problem. Just being with them in the moment and showing our support in a compassionate way—this is relationship too.

We All Need Different Types of Attention

All people do not need the same amounts or types of attention all the time. What a child needs can depend on a child's birth order in the family, personality, genes, culture, or life experiences. One morning when I was working on this chapter in my favorite coffee shop in Philadelphia, a woman was seated next to me working on her computer. She began chatting with me about the trouble she was having with Internet access. One thing led to another, and soon she was asking me what I was working on. I explained it was a book about children needing attention. As is often the case when I tell people what I am writing about, she immediately began sharing her experiences with her children. She described how different they were in their expression of need for attention. She said that her eldest seemed to be able to "get on with it," not requiring much attention at all, whereas her middle child seemed to need more support, specifically her praise and acknowledgment.

Making even small changes in our lives from how we were brought up or what was modeled for us by our parents can be hard. I was taught to stifle even those emotions of joy or pride in what I had accomplished. Recently when friends visited me in Israel after not seeing me for many years and were excited to learn about my accomplishments in my professional life, my mother interrupted their questions and exclaimed, "Before we get excited about the *genius* in the room, let's remember who created her," thereby immediately taking the attention away from me. It was so effective that I immediately felt ashamed, as if I had done something wrong to feel joy and pride that my old friends were thinking highly of my accomplishments. We need attention for the good and the bad. We need different types of attention for different types of emotions, expressions, accomplishments—or even for just being present. We feel valued if other people notice us when we are young children. Even as adults we derive pleasure from being noticed. We are social beings and depend on social interactions.

Only in recent years have I accepted that I enjoy receiving attention despite the fact that it still causes me discomfort or feelings of guilt and shame because I don't feel deserving of it. Asking for and receiving attention remain a painful process. I describe "changing my emotional script" in more detail in my book *"Don't Get So Upset!"* (2008). I am an advocate for children who need clear, concrete messages that they are wanted, acceptable, and even lovable in spite of the fact and also especially *because* they want our attention. I do not want them to experience the emotional bind that I lived through as a young child.

Practicing What I Preach

This past summer in the afternoons, I took care of Benya, a four-month-old infant, for a dear friend who had to go back to work way too early for either of them to bear. The experience was amazing for me and especially meaningful because I was working on this book. And so, in the mornings I would read, reflect, and write about children and adults needing and wanting attention. In the afternoons, I would practice with the infant what I had been working on in the morning. This went on for a couple of months. Needless to say, it was an emotionally intense time for me: processing my childhood soon after my mother died, writing a book that I felt is important to share with teachers and parents, and especially taking care of an infant.

Most days, soon after the child arrived, he would look around the house as I carried him into the living room area. As he recognized that this was not his home, he would start with a sad whimper, which then became an angry cry. This was not fair, he seemed to tell me. He would so have preferred to be nestled with his mother in the pouch she carried him in when she was with him—close to her beating heart, familiar smells, and her nursing breasts. Also, he had spent all morning with his loving and devoted father, who had been completely focused on him, playing with him, going for walks, and holding him close for naps. Why did he have to leave all that for this strange place? After a few minutes of crying, I would try to help him sleep on the bed I had created for him on my couch. I would lay him down and pat and stroke him, cooing softly and telling him everything would be all right. Sometimes that would work. Other times his cries would become stronger, more forceful. Clearly, he was not pleased with this idea. Then I would bundle him in his swaddling blanket of muslin cotton, hold him close to my chest, and rock him to sleep in my arms. His crying would abate, and he would sigh deeply with relief. Once asleep, I could lay him down for his afternoon nap, although many times I sat with him on the couch nestled in my arms. It was an opportunity for me, too, to rest and experience the warmth of his little body.

During this time, I read an article that I had found posted by an early childhood colleague on her Facebook page. It was called "Screaming to Sleep, Part One: The Moral Imperative to End 'Cry It Out'" (Wright Glenn 2015). At the top of the page of the article was a photograph of an infant crying uncontrollably with a caption that read, "Cry It Out, also known as 'controlled crying,' is an 'extinction method' of ending—'extinguishing'—the cuing for attention, help, nourishment, hydration, support, and loving, physical comfort that is programmed into the biology of young mammals" (Wright Glenn 2015).

I read the horrific description of infants covered in tears, sweat, and sometimes vomit, exhausting themselves out of despair, anger, and panic and then forcing themselves into sleep. Looking at my friend's child sleeping peacefully, trusting, and sighing with relief in my arms, I wondered, "Why on earth would people knowingly and intentionally isolate, ignore, or punish *anyone* cuing for attention, support, or loving physical comfort?" I came to the conclusion that to be able to do this to an infant, first a person must be ignorant about child development in general, and brain development specifically. Second, they must have developed a harsh worldview through their own early childhood experiences. And third, of course, there are many complex reasons for how any one person interacts with another.

For the past fifteen years or so, my husband and I have had cats. Currently we have the two I mentioned earlier, Oscar and Mimi. Friends and relatives throughout the years have remarked to me about how well behaved our cats are, the ones we have now and the cats we used to have, Molly and Ada. Our cats don't litter outside their litter box like some cats do, never take food from countertops, and—wait for it—they actually come to me when I sit on the floor tapping their hairbrush. They lie in front of me and purr calmly when I brush them every two weeks or so. They also lie completely still, purring in my husband's arms, when I clip their nails. Strange as it may sound to some of you, I believe my cats are well behaved because since they were kittens, I have related to them with respect. Over the years, all the various cats in our home came from different cat families, and all but one were rescue kittens. So they have not come as siblings from the same litters and have not been genetically similar.

Relating to them with respect means, for example, that when they come up to sniff my food, I show it to them and allow them to come close. Most of the time they are not interested in what I am eating once I have shown it to them. I talk to them gently and take an interest in their habits, always arranging for someone who is kind and respectful to care for them when we are away. I try to treat them with compassion. I can't really put myself in their shoes because I am not a cat! But I can treat them with respect nevertheless. Cats need attention too. That reminds me of when I first brought home Oscar and Mimi. I wrote about them in my blog:

> Well, now I have *two* kittens in the house and am faced with early education challenges. I find myself confronted with situations that require attitudes and behaviors from me—many, which I suggest or expect from the pre- or in-service teachers I instruct or mentor. Naturally I understand that a kitten is not a human child. Or do I? I wonder. These little creatures were raised for many weeks in a large cage together, the remaining duo from a litter of six. Mimi is sturdy, strong, and healthy. She is rambunctious and smart, eats voraciously, and constantly is at play with everything she can lay her paws on. Oscar is tiny, tender, gentle, and fragile. He seems to wobble as he wanders cautiously through the house. My sister, Sue, described him as wearing his "battle dress" as he slinks around prepared to defend himself at any moment from any incoming danger, namely, his sister, Mimi. She charges him and urges him to

rough and tumble, but he refuses and subsides into the background. Often, we find him hunkered down next to one of the heating units, and he sleeps, it seems, all day and all night.

I go in and out of *parental* panic. Should I intervene on Oscar's behalf? Or discipline dear little Mimi? And what does that mean? "*To discipline Mimi.*" Can one really set boundaries for a cat? For example, what happens when I am out of the house and they learn to live together, which they have done already in their earliest kittenhood within the confines of their cage? At times, I adore Mimi as she runs around with her red ball, chasing and tumbling with it, and then running towards me with her little bandy legs, carrying the ball in her mouth, expecting me to throw it for her to "fetch," again and

> again. There are times when I experience frustration when she charges her vulnerable, little brother, while understanding, at the very same time, that they have to work out their own dynamics and power structures as two cats living in the same house. And there I go again and again—round and round, confused and anxious, not knowing what to do!
>
> True enough, it surely presses all kinds of personal buttons to see Oscar as the underdog (cat?), a victim to marginalization and working hard to be invisible—out of Mimi's range. I have to admit that I find myself identifying with him. And, on the other hand, that feeling makes me as mad as a hatter. Because I have been working on myself in therapy for years in order *not* to feel like that. Indeed, I have made a conscious decision to take all kinds of emotional stands for me recently, and no longer feel like a victim. No indeed. Just the opposite. I feel empowered and so much more confident. I realize, too, that dear sweet little Mimi is not the "bad guy (girl?)." Just a little kitty with developmental needs of her own.

And so, I conclude that Oscar's cat behavior, as he works within the power structure of his relationship with sister, Mimi, has absolutely nothing to do with who I am nor how I perceive myself. Wow! Therapeutic opportunity! Perhaps finding these two cats was the very thing I needed to remind me about myself and how I view early education. That is, that our own emotional development affects how we relate to and interact with children and families. Plain and simple. We have an awesome responsibility to work on ourselves psychologically when we develop relationships with other human beings—or cats for that matter (Jacobson 2013).

Chapter 3

Self-Regulation

For children, intense emotions are like a dark forest at night. Trees rustle in the wind, bats circle above, and all manner of insects crawl along the ground, but in the darkness they are impossible to see, let alone understand. The brain starts making associations, and the child becomes overwhelmed with dark imaginings. When we use discipline methods like time-out, we essentially usher our kids into the woods and just leave them there in the darkness. More, we actually tell them to sit there silently and not to move no matter what they experience so that they can "reflect" on their actions. —*Roger Thompson (2014)*

I COULD NOT HELP CRYING silently one morning as I started my drive to work. The morning started out peacefully enough. The usual: feeding of the cats, playing my few Internet Scrabble moves with my nephew and a few Facebook friends, yoga exercises, meditation, and a refreshing shower. I boiled an egg and made a lox and cream cheese sandwich for the road, and after imbibing what seemed like a million vitamins and a potassium-filled banana, I headed out to the university. At nine in the morning, the traffic had slowed to a comfortable pace, and I turned down a side street that would lead me out to the main highway. As the car pulled around to the left, my eyes attached themselves suddenly to a woman slapping a three-year-old child so hard that she fell to the sidewalk on her back. It literally took my breath away. I gasped out loud and pulled the car to the side of the road, unsure how to react. Thank goodness, the little girl was wearing a down jacket, which must have cushioned her fall. The woman dragged her up by her arm and pushed her to walk ahead. The child was sobbing.

As I tried to pull myself together while tears welled up in my eyes, I noticed that the woman was holding a toddler on her hip and seemed to have tied to her front a baby covered by a blanket shielded from the cold. The woman was clearly overwhelmed. I did not assume she was the children's mother, although it looked as if she was. I drove slowly forward, wiping away my tears and staring at the little group as they walked slowly along the sidewalk. By now the woman had noticed I was staring, and she put her hand out to the little girl, who was still weeping. She pushed her ahead slightly more gently. I seemed paralyzed, stuck, and somehow unable to drive away. I did not want to leave the child, and yet there was nothing I could do. I was in hell, and I noticed that I completely identified with the sobbing three-year-old. Finally, with the woman glaring at my staring interference, I pulled myself together and drove away.

As I drove, I wept silently on and off, all the while thinking of the little girl as she was slapped down onto the sidewalk. I was kicking myself for not having stopped the car and run out to help the woman, who seemed so overwhelmed. Why did I not come to the rescue, just to show all of them that somebody cared? Instead, I sat frozen, wallowing in pain and grief at all the insult, violence, and hurt that small child was enduring on this wintry morning.

I remembered how a couple of the participants at the keynote I had presented the Saturday before had stated that hitting children was fine in certain circumstances, that the Bible declared it so: "Spare the rod and spoil the child." They debated with me about that when I put up a slide that read, "It's never okay to hit a child. You don't have to hurt me to teach me." I considered the life of the young woman that morning as she carried two small children on her body and needed the third one to walk alongside obediently. As the oldest child, the little girl, at three years of age, had to give up all rights to her childhood needs: in this instance, to dawdle along the way, being in the moment to stop and look at things as they appeared. If she was "needing attention," she certainly deserved it, and she definitely needed her mother's love as much as the other two clinging to the woman's body. How lonely and cold that morning must have felt for that three-year-old child. How hurtful adults must seem to her.

And then again, how could the woman be a good mother to all three needy souls simultaneously? What if all she knew was beatings and pain from when *she* was a child? I was emotionally and intellectually overwhelmed as I drove along the highway to work. After about half an hour, I managed to stop crying, and twenty minutes later I was pulling into the driveway at the university. I parked my car and walked thoughtfully into the building. My body seemed to ache in all sorts of places, as if I had been on a long hike.

Self-Regulation or Punishment?

For me, this chapter is probably one of the most important in this book. For it is the very idea of self-regulation and self-soothing that is at the source of our aversion to children needing our attention. In other words, "Kids, get on with it! . . . Do not *disrupt* our routine. We have much more important issues to deal with right now. Reading, math, assessments, administrators stopping by to see how well I run my classroom. It must not seem *messy* or *chaotic*. I must look like I have *control* of my classroom. So . . . self-regulate, self-soothe, and please, whatever you do, *do not need me*! I have much more important things to deal with here." And yet in any society that includes different and unique human beings, relationships are going to be fraught with challenges, chaos, and, yes, a lot of messiness.

In a democratic or what some might like to term a "civilized society," we long for a sense of order and responsibility, where everyone knows their place and people consider others responsibly. If we are "self-regulated" and abide by the rules of conduct, there will be no mess, infraction, disruption, or intrusion into personal space. What we forget is that societies of all descriptions are made up of human beings with different feelings and needs.

So where do I begin to talk about self-regulation? This is the latest buzzword for young children learning some kind of self-control when it comes to behavior and classroom management. The intent behind the expression is admirable. To succeed academically and emotionally, young children need to learn how to live in society by understanding its norms and rules (McClelland, Diaz, and Lewis 2016). We also want them to become contributing members of our society—our adult world. Somehow, however, teaching children to self-regulate becomes punitive, as teachers and parents take on a behaviorist approach using punishments and rewards. Instead, self-regulation becomes about pleasing people and stifling emotions: "I will do anything, just please don't ignore me." What about empathy and compassion, or making a stand for social justice? How do we learn these characteristics and skills by pleasing people?

For example, let's say a child doesn't get what we are telling her the first time. Perhaps she needs it repeated a few times. I know I am like that when something makes me anxious or insecure. I might need the other person to repeat for me so that I feel safe in that context. Saying to me, "How many times must I tell you that?" will only make me feel like I am burdening the other person—that there must be something wrong with me because I need it repeated. I would rather remain silent and please the teacher than ask her to repeat it one more time and appear to be a nag, a whiner, or, worse still, a burden on her time.

At the core of my beliefs about working with children is that children need us to make a stand for them emotionally. At so many levels I feel this, but it probably started when I was a child and no one protected me emotionally—no one made a stand for me. I have since developed what I describe as an *on-your-side-ness* for children. I give children the benefit of the doubt. I realize that while children need our support and for us to relate to them, validating and accepting their feelings, at the same time adults are *recovering children* who need their own attention and relationships too. We all needed someone to make a stand for us emotionally when we were growing up. If we did not receive it, how can we learn to feel the same way toward others? This question is central to my work with children and teachers. How do we balance it so that everyone gets their emotional needs met, especially when children are unable to make a stand for themselves except in ways that adults often abhor and reject through humiliation or aggressive reaction?

Making Children Our Priority

I want children to feel like they are our priority: at home, in classrooms, and in society at large. Each time I make a child my priority, I am able to work on healing the child within me. I relive what it could have and should have been like for me growing up, and indeed, I make an emotional stand for myself over and over again—through my advocacy for young children. Self-regulation works if it is learned as a positive experience—when it makes sense and when the child is emotionally capable of understanding the value of self-control. It does not help the child develop mental health in the long run if it works as a form of repression out of fear and longing. I am a testament to that!

So, as adults, teachers, and parents, how do we determine when a child is emotionally capable of understanding the adult objectives of self-regulation? Some children may behave in what seem like oppositional ways, but they are actually severely anxious. For example, I think of a five-year-old who had been moved from foster home to foster home—feeling he was to blame for each abandonment—arriving in a school classroom and finding it so very difficult to self-regulate. This poor child was an emotional bundle of self-worthlessness. In the end, not only was he expelled from the school, out of the teacher's frustration that he would not conform to their strict rules, but he was moved to yet another foster home. When in his life would a compassionate adult hold still long enough to give him enough of the attention he craved to break the cycle of abandonment?

How do young children express to us their fear of abandonment? Their longing for more of us? How do we gauge what is the right amount for each person? In many cases, it is mostly according to our own emotional needs, external pressures, childhood memories, and the ways in which we learned to survive when we were children. Indeed, we are as subjective and as biased as can be. There is no one right way for everyone, and we are tested over and over again when there are strong emotions. Life is as serious for children as it is for adults. We laugh at little children a lot—all too often because we think of them as "cute," when, in fact, children's lives are serious. We trivialize children's self-expression, thereby teaching them that their thoughts, feelings, and opinions are less important than those of adults. Trivializing is a form of attention too, just as humiliation and aggression are. All of those methods teach children something about who they are—and how we perceive them. Because of their egocentric stage of development, they will assume the blame; that is, they take it on themselves and think there must be something wrong with them when we reject them.

Seeking Attention as a Disruption

We have the power and opportunity as adults to confront our painful memories. It is up to us each time we interact with children in emotional situations to choose a form of attention giving that helps children learn how worthwhile and lovable they are. When children are timed-out or punished in isolation for strong feelings they are experiencing and expressing, they learn that their emotions are wrong, that they are bad and worthless. As they learn about stifling emotions, they are deprived of learning an essential skill for social-emotional development: acquiring an understanding and vocabulary about complicated emotions—which is crucial for effective and healthy human relationships. How on earth can they learn compassion, empathy, or emotional understanding when they are sitting alone somewhere in isolation, rejected and abandoned because we are giving them the message that they are not worth the emotional trouble, effort, or time?

Recently, while considering subscribing to a program of educational videos for teaching students at our university, I watched a sample video where the facilitators suggested that adults needed to be playful with children (ChildCareExchange, Ed.flicks). They admitted to not being trained educators. Yet their ideas about being playful were as appropriate as could be. Indeed, they discovered that by playing with children, they allowed themselves to form a relationship with each child. They discovered that over time this was helping children who had suffered trauma in their home environments. In the course of the discussion, the facilitators said that instead of children "disrupting the class," they could be given playful activities. A worthy idea! However, I took exception to the expression of "disrupting the class." I understand that as teachers we have an agenda, and that when children stray from our plan, we feel like it is a disruption. I would prefer, however, that we learn to see different behaviors as children's different emotional needs being met. While we are not trained counselors or social workers, as teachers we can become aware that children are not all on the same page emotionally when we don't see these behaviors as disruptions.

In all the books and articles that I have read about classroom management and discipline strategies, terms like *disruption* are bandied about freely. Especially as something wrong, something that has to be averted at all costs. The concept of "disruption" is as fraught with negative connotation as could be. Of course we do not want people "disrupting" our lives. But when we are talking about working with young children, let's take that a step back and delve deeper into understanding what we mean by "disruption." It means we have some sort of plan that must take place without diversion. If we are led down a different path, we may become "out of control," or dangerous things will happen, perhaps? When I am giving a presentation on a certain topic, I often find myself diverting to different ideas and associations along the way. I have an outline, a plan, and even a PowerPoint presentation to guide me. However, as I speak and others comment, interrupt, or share their ideas and emotions, I find I must go in different directions to accommodate and include them. I do not see them as a *disruption* to my plan. On the contrary, they enhance it and give it depth, and I learn new things about human emotion, the lives of others, and the human condition overall. I develop more and more compassion and acceptance of the diversity of humanity. These diversions are enormously beneficial in the long run.

The same applies to teaching young children in a classroom. Of course we have a plan, an agenda. But along the way, ideas and feelings of the children in this mini-society of human beings—the classroom—must disrupt our attention to something larger, more complex, and essential to a bigger picture of how people live together in community. We learn together not only how to read or write, but how we communicate with one another, how we care about each other, and how we can all contribute to the whole community we are living in by stopping to listen to one another with empathy and compassion. In the end, we return to our original plan with newer, fresher ideas, feeling strengthened by our collective humanity. The word *disruption* should be banned from our understanding about discipline and learning how to live with one another in a compassionate and productive society. We should instead see *disruption* as an *opportunity* to widen our emotional understanding of one another, to learn something new about one another. We should seize the opportunity with excitement, even joy.

Time-Outs Stifle Feelings

> And make no mistake: putting a child on a time-out chair is punishment. A child in time-out is not thinking, "I am going to be a better child because of this experience. I am glad Teacher made me sit here." The child is angry with the teacher for the embarrassment experienced during the conflict. The child is angry at the one who got him into trouble. The child is feeling rejected by the classroom community and reinforced in a negative self-image. Not having been taught other ways to handle conflict, the child is left with only survival-behavior reactions.
>
> —Dan Gartrell (2016)

We have an obligation to young children to guide them into an understanding of self-regulation and negotiation of feelings and needs. Casting them out, expelling them, sending them to time-out, rewarding and punishing them into submission only teaches them that feelings are bad and are to be stifled. Our responsibility is to give them the skills to develop an emotional vocabulary and to learn how to listen and interpret others' feelings and ideas. This process is complex but important for the acceptance of the diversity of ideas and feelings and of our humanity. It is more sophisticated than "I'll give you a sticker each time you obey." Children are capable of complexity. We are the ones who dumb down everything for them instead of expanding their emotional understanding and facilitating complex communication.

The Importance of Confronting Painful Memories

And so now I must bring the issue directly back to us—the adults in the room. How did we learn about emotional complexity, compassion, and the negotiation of our feelings and needs? And how can we facilitate a complex emotional vocabulary and interaction with children when we have no experience with it ourselves? When all we know is punishments and rewards in our own lives, we often find it difficult—almost impossible—to shift our understanding of discipline and self-regulation to something more humane and complex. We learn about self-regulation through relationships with others. When we trust others and feel emotionally safe, we find it much easier to self-soothe and wait our turn, knowing that we will be respected along the way. When we are humiliated, rejected, and abandoned, we do not learn anything about trusting others or feeling safe. We become constantly on the lookout for something bad to happen to us to confirm our worthlessness to others.

As I write this, I am reminded of my own childhood and what I learned about the importance of stifling my feelings. Indeed, when I did try to share them, it caused my mother much angst and distress. So I realized early on that to survive as a young child in my family, I would need to hold back my emotions and self-soothe. What this taught me was a sense of worthlessness and loneliness. I learned to numb my longing for validation and acknowledgment, which I have only recently, in my late sixties, allowed myself to feel. Following my mother's death at the age of ninety-nine, my grief culminated in a deep sense of longing for the mothering that I simply never had. This stifled sense of longing clouded many of my decisions as I grew up and entered my marital relationships, and it even helped me choose career paths. In short, I know firsthand the harm it can do to children for the rest of their lives when they are taught to repress feelings out of fear for their survival. I find that nowadays I am emotionally exhausted from going it alone. All these years, it has been an enormous strain on me and has interfered with my asking for help from others. Now that I am able to reach out for emotional help from time to time, my relationships are enhanced and strengthened, and I am beginning to develop a stronger sense of self-worth.

I wonder if some children learn, as I did, that if they give up their selves and needs, their mother will finally notice or acknowledge them. In other words, holding back the emotions and doing only what is required may perhaps cause the teacher or parent to notice a child for her goodness and cooperation. Sadly, that does not really work either. Because the more repressed and compliant a person becomes, the less need there is to make the effort to notice her. Adults are focused on their own needs and are jolted to respond to those who have learned to clamor for our attention.

In my work with children and teachers, I am usually drawn to the children who are at either extreme: the silent, withdrawn, compliant ones, and the ones who bombastically bring all the attention to themselves constantly. Be good and thankfully go unnoticed while secretly longing to be acknowledged and validated (so secretly that the child is usually unaware of her longing). Or make as much noise as possible so that people yell at or even hit her, so that she knows she exists and is not ignored.

In a TED talk, Sir Kenneth Robinson described what happened to Dame Gillian Lynne when she was eight years old (Robinson 2007). Lynne is a renowned choreographer, whom Robinson interviewed. She told him about being fidgety and "disruptive" at school in the 1930s. When her mother took her to a doctor, he questioned her mother about her problems and issues and then told Lynne that he and her mother needed to leave the room to talk privately. As they left, he turned on the radio. Then he told her mother to watch her daughter alone in the room with the radio. Lynne began to move with the music. The doctor declared that Lynne was not *sick*. She was a dancer! Dame Gillian Lynne went on to be a world-renowned dancer and choreographer. Robinson suggested that in today's education system, Lynne might have been diagnosed with ADHD because she was unable to self-regulate. While Robinson was telling a story about recognizing children's capacity for creativity, I realized that he was also talking about relationship: getting to know the whole child and why she was fidgety and unable to sit still. In Lynne's case, dancing was an avenue for self-expression. But another child may be unable to sit still because of emotional anxiety. In any event, why do we make young children sit still for long periods of time? If we understand anything at all about child development, we know that they need to be busy with hands-on, relevant curriculum that expands their minds and challenges their emotional potential as well as their creativity.

Intolerance for Nonconformist Behavior

While I understand that children need to learn to function in an adult society without always getting their needs met, I am concerned that when adults focus on self-regulation so obsessively, it is often more about the teacher's or parent's personal agenda or anxieties. For teachers, how they were treated when they were children may not be all that affects their decisions and interactions with children in the classroom; they may also be worried about their professional survival as teachers. Teacher accountability in recent years has created high anxiety for educators about retaining their positions. Their days are fraught with paperwork and assessments of children, and there are not enough hands in the room for them to be able to interact appropriately with each child. I have been in schools, though, where an extra aide helps out with children who *disrupt* the day's routine. I imagined that their role was to intervene and learn about the needs of children who were not able to sit still through the rote and structured lessons on boring topics, like the calendar and weather. What I actually witnessed, however, was more time-outs and rejection from even those specialized aides.

Intolerance of nonconformist behaviors in children is as high as can be in classrooms that I witness each semester when I visit my student teachers or student interns doing their practicums in schools as requirements for their teaching certification. Over the years, these same students have shared what they experienced during their internship. Some found these experiences difficult because what they witnessed conflicted considerably with what they were learning from me in class. They expressed frustration with how the teachers wanted these very young children to learn to self-regulate. One described an incident in a preschool classroom:

> Today "K" broke my heart. She was singing to herself during circle time and did not recite the date with the rest of the class. Mrs. H. made K recite it alone. K barely squeaked the words out and Mrs. H. kept yelling at her to use her "big girl" voice. I was horrified. . . . K was in tears by the time she got through the date. . . . Her attention remained unfocused all day; even when she was removed from circle, she did not face the class and kept singing. On the way back from gym, I heard her singing about playing all together and going on their way back to class. (Jacobson 2008)

Another described discipline in the older infant room:

> For example, when the oldest one, H, would let out what they called the "ostrich cry," they knew it was a cry for attention, rather than a pain cry or a hungry cry. So the main teacher would say to her in a stern voice, "Stop!" H would go to the teachers' legs and pull on them to be picked up, but the teacher would tell her they won't pick her up until she stops crying, so H would yell out more. H's designated teacher would want to hold her so bad and sometimes would sit on the floor just so H could crawl onto her lap so she could hold her. Her designated teacher would hug her tight and rock her back and forth, and then H would rejuvenate and go run off

> and play. The head teacher would say a remark afterwards like she needs to stop doing that; that's why you can't pick her up. I wanted to hold her so bad because she was just crying out for a hug, but I didn't feel comfortable enough to interject like H's designated teacher did.

When describing an older infant who did not like to nap, the teachers assumed it was because at home she slept in a family bed with her sister, mother, and father. The student described what happened after the teacher told the child it was naptime and she began to cry:

> She continued to cry, and after such a prolonged period of time [of rocking her in a stroller], they put her in time-out in which she was in the stroller and facing the corner of the wall.

How does an older infant who fears sleeping alone in a crib learn to trust or develop a feeling of self-worth by being isolated with her face to the wall during naptime? Does she learn to self-soothe as she stifles feelings of fear and loneliness? Or does she feel rejected and abandoned and learn not to trust adults in the future? One of the reasons toddlers bite, writes Gretchen Kinnell, is because they "want and need more attention" (Kinnell 2008, 10). And, in fact, they certainly receive attention if they bite. Kinnell suggests that they would rather "get the attention associated with biting—even if it is not pleasant—than get little or no attention" (10). What is significant about Kinnell's finding is that "if we purposefully withhold attention, toddlers may bite even more" (11).

Recently, I read an opinion piece in the *New York Times* that described research that shows human beings need to feel liked or popular (Prinstein 2017). Indeed, they seek these feelings out in different ways. The researcher found that people's feelings about being lonely or disconnected could predict their life span. The article went on to say the following:

> More surprising is just how powerful this effect can be. Dr. Holt-Lunstad found that people [adults] who had larger networks of friends had a 50 percent increased chance of survival by the end of the study they were in. And those who had good-quality relationships had a 91 percent higher survival rate. This suggests that being unpopular increases our chance of death more strongly than obesity, physical inactivity or binge drinking. (Prinstein 2017)

Sometimes the most challenging children become the most unpopular because children observe the teacher's frustrations and learn to fear them because there seems no way to solve the problems. But sometimes the most challenging children have not been given a chance to learn how to behave differently because from year to year they receive the harshest punishments as a way of "fixing a problem" that teachers have no time, training, or understanding for how to solve.

In a study spanning five decades about simple spanking that was not considered abuse per se, researchers found that "the more children are spanked, the more likely they are to defy their parents and to experience increased anti-social behavior, aggression, mental health problems and cognitive difficulties" (UT News 2016). Standard disciplinary methods are rooted in a behaviorist philosophy that believes human behavior is determined solely by consequences or punishments. This belief system holds for young and older children. In fact, some researchers are finding that these methods, instead of resolving challenging behaviors, may be making them worse (Lewis 2015). In fact, if we consider that behavioral challenges are often brought about by stress and trauma, and harsh punishments make the behaviors worse, it makes sense to seek out new ways to negotiate behaviors that challenge us (Perry 2016). And I believe that because harsh punishments are not helping to solve behavioral problems, more emphasis is lately being put on social-emotional development and even teaching about emotions in schools (Bierman, Greenberg, and Abenavoli 2017; Harper 2016; Rubenstein 2017; Tominey et al. 2017; Zins et al. 2004).

How We Were Treated as Children Influences Our Behaviors

As much as we may learn and understand best practices for children, when it comes to self-regulation, needing attention, and discipline in general, the way we were treated as children often influences our behaviors and interactions. Recently a teacher of young children wrote me an email after she finished reading my book *"Don't Get So Upset!"* (2008). She wrote that she had chosen to read the book because of "struggles" she was having with a child aged three and a half:

> In the past few months his tantrums have gone from normal "life as a three-year-old is hard" to explosive and emotionally charged. Lately I have been able to be honest with myself and notice that I am uncomfortable with these outbursts because I have the same response to disappointment, anger, frustration, etc., but I learned early on to quash down those emotions and any outward expression of them. I have spent the past decade working through my issues and deepening my own self-awareness in therapy and on my own, so your message resonated with me. . . . Yesterday and today I have spent time reading and reflecting, sitting with my discomfort, exploring those rabbit trail ideas that could lead to more self-discovery. It has not been enjoyable . . . but I'm also allowing myself to be vulnerable and talk about my discoveries. . . . I can't say that I have had an earth-shattering "AHA!" moment, because that would be too easy, wouldn't it? Yet I now feel ready to sit with those feelings of discomfort and anger when they come while I am with [the three-year-old

> child], and to embrace him and myself with compassion as we both work through things.

This teacher wrote to me specifically about her emotions (even though they were uncomfortable for her to face), and after self-reflection she was able to be more intentional and compassionate both with the three-year-old child and herself. Instead of resorting to old patterns of behavior that are not helpful in resolving struggles within and without, we have the option to change how we react and behave. The choice is ours.

In chapter 5, I will discuss more about strategies for giving or withholding attention, including reminders about child development, the best way to organize and design the physical environment, and things to consider about giving praise. However, no matter what external solutions we choose, the manner in which we implement our discipline strategies will depend on our mind-set. Our mind was set when we were young children, influenced by our earliest experiences and interactions with significant adults in our lives. "Un-setting" our minds and trying out different approaches often conflict with what we were taught early on in a deeply emotional way, so much so that it becomes impossible to even imagine that doing things another way could work.

Remembering a Traumatic Event

I wake up and lie in my bed looking out at the cool of a summer morning. One stray tear rolls down my cheek. I think of an eight-year-old child unable to sleep. Her stomach is rumbling, and she feels nauseous. She calls out to her mother, who is asleep down the stairs and to the right, in a room with a closed door alongside a long, dark living room. The child is feeling very poorly and confused about her bodily feelings, and she starts to panic. So she calls more loudly, fearing that her mother can't hear, but at the same time anxious about disturbing her mother, stepfather, and newly born baby brother, also asleep behind that closed door. Her mother thunders up the stairs and shouts at her, telling her to go to sleep. She is disturbing everyone. "Stop making a performance!" her mother yells. The child cries and begs her not to leave the room. Her bodily sensations are frightening her. She gets out of her bed and runs to her mother, who slaps her, grabs her arm, and flings her around the room over and over again. "Be quiet! Go to sleep! What's the matter with you! You're disturbing everyone!" her mother shouts. Now the little girl is terrified. A policeman in the neighborhood saves the day. Walking around the corner, hearing the mother's shouting and the child's crying in fear, he comes to the window and knocks on it. When the mother opens it, he asks if everything is all right. She says that it is, and he wanders off. The mother turns to the girl with what seems like an enormous angry face. "Now look what you've done! Go to sleep!" She hisses aggressively and hatefully under her breath and storms out of the room and down the stairs.

I described this story a little differently in *"Don't Get So Upset!"* (2008). The little girl was me, and as some of you may remember, the end of the story came with relief the next morning when I went to the bathroom (and this might gross you out!) and my mother, wailing in shock, pulled out of me a long tapeworm. After that, she took me to the hospital. The hospital was run by Irish nuns, who took care of me with great kindness. I remember my hospital room as airy and sunny, and I did not want to go home from there. The relief came because even at age eight I realized that when I behaved so badly as to disturb everyone in the house, including the policeman, in fact I hadn't been bad that night—I was just ill.

As I lay in bed thinking about that event, I remembered the story more viscerally than when I described it a decade ago. Much more in touch with my emotions now, this time I remembered my *feelings* of terror and anguish that night. I tried so hard to be good and just sleep, to *self-regulate,* but my fears and bodily sensations took over. I longed for my mother to hold me and tell me everything would be all right, but everything about her behavior toward me, including her yells, slapping, flinging me around the room, and hatred in her eyes, told me what a bad person I was. I was even to blame for disturbing the policeman, who wandered through the neighborhood!

At eight years old, children have already developed a sense of self-identity. At that time, I was already acutely aware that I was in the way of my mother's new life with my stepfather and their newborn baby. I already had enough knowledge to know I was a burden. For that very reason, I started out afraid when I called out for my mother, because I knew that I would get into some kind of trouble. However, my physical condition was more frightening, and so I did, in fact, call out. Imagine how terrifying punishments are for children who are four years old—or two and a half—when they reach out for attention and are put in time-out in the corner or left to sit strapped into small chairs because they can't finish their food. In early childhood they are at the beginning stages of developing a self-identity. They are egocentric and feel to blame for everything. They are unaware that they are not to blame for adult outbursts.

Believe me, I knew how to self-regulate by the time I was eight years old. It didn't matter how physically ill I was feeling, I knew well enough not to call out again for my mother when she left the room. I knew I would have to go it alone that night (as I did then on for the rest of my childhood and much of my adulthood):

> Still unable to sleep, I stumbled as softly as I could down the stairs and lay on the sofa in the living room, as near as possible to her closed bedroom door. My mother's newborn baby was asleep in their bedroom down the stairs, all the way through the living room to the front of the house. At the time, we lived behind my stepfather's store, a long, dark warehouse turned

> into a home. My mother had painted the back wall a deep shade of red, and as there were no windows, I always remember the living room as being long, dark, and ominous. As I lay down I sensed a large, thick, pungent, pale green cobweb-like cloud above my head, spreading out over the ceiling with layers falling down and around to hover just above my body. I was terrified and lay awake trembling, not daring to call out, keeping my eyes fixed on that imaginary cloud until the morning light drove it away. (Jacobson 2008)

I look back to Roger Thompson's words at the beginning of this chapter and am amazed at how he captures the feelings of a young child put in time-out or some type of isolation as a punishment. I might not have been in a dark forest, as he describes, but where I lay, it was dark and ominous with a *large, thick, pungent, pale green cobweb-like cloud.* Do we have to reject, abandon, and leave children to their fears when we teach them to self-regulate? Or can we realize they are all, every one, human beings full of emotions, anxieties, and confusions who need us to guide them along with compassion and understanding?

Chapter 4

When Teachers Face Themselves

There is much in the professional work of a good therapist that can also be made part of the work of the teacher. . . . This will require teachers to face personal issues in their own lives—through therapy or discussion of "personal and emotional issues"—in a manner that differs from the usual academic work. —*Arthur T. Jersild (1955)*

THE PHRASE "KNOW THYSELF" GOES BACK as far as the ancient Greeks. One of the meanings of it was that learning about worldly matters was dependent on knowing about oneself first. My shelves are bursting with books that describe how teachers could or should do things: managing behavior by using this or that technique, adding play to the curriculum, designing lesson plans, setting up the physical environment, conducting observations, creating an antibias curriculum, and so many more. However, leafing through the pages of these resources, I find little information about how to go about "knowing thyself." It makes me wonder what kind of antibias curriculum someone might develop if they are uncomfortable with differences in others, or how they might manage behavior if they were severely punished as a child and are uncomfortable or at a loss when reacting to children's challenging behaviors. In fact, for the most part, educators write about teaching as if it is an act, something we practice without much focus on our emotions or how our personal experiences affect what we do with children and families.

Indeed, these days some people even think that we don't need to be physically present in the classroom to teach others. We can interact through cyberspace and teach online, leaving the element of relationships to a distant learning model. This way provides even less room for the need to understand or "know thyself." When we distance ourselves physically from others, we may no longer be concerned with the conscious or unconscious nonverbal reactions we have, including glances, smiles, grimaces, the proximity of our bodies, touch, and so on.

A few years ago, I heard a panel of professors reflecting about different aspects of Reggio Emilia curriculum methodologies and their place in American early childhood education. One of the panelists described Swedish schools that have been inspired by Reggio Emilia's emergent curriculum philosophy. She reported that professors of education in Sweden believe that when teachers work to incorporate an open-ended curriculum, it is critical for them to think in professional, sociocultural, and, most especially, private ways about why they feel this or that way about children (Ferholt et al. 2015). She described a process of self-reflection that never ends.

In my experience as a campus children's center director and university teacher educator, teachers in America have difficulty with open-endedness, especially because of their own childhood experiences, which were influenced by emotional repression, closed questioning, intense structure, and even harshness. In other words, when they were children they did not experience open-endedness, an emerging type of curriculum in their classrooms, or a safe emotional environment. Undergraduate and graduate students in my classes, for example, report feeling confused, overwhelmed, and even anxious if their assignments are not linked to detailed rubrics that inform them precisely how to do whatever is required of them. They also express feeling uncomfortable, confused, or at a loss when they attempt an emerging, exploratory model like the curriculum at Reggio schools. Therefore, to revise our style of teaching or to incorporate new ways of interacting with children, we must consider engaging in a process of self-reflection that is specifically related to our memories of early childhood about how we experienced how we were taught.

Understanding Emotions

> In our society we undervalue emotion. It's often viewed as a nuisance. Words are frequently applied to it like "sappy," "mushy," or "schmaltzy." Emotion is often thought of as childish, effeminate, or weak. It's considered the antithesis of thought. We have the tendency to assume that smart people aren't emotional people, and emotional people aren't smart. The reality is that the smartest people are those who use their emotions to help them think and who use their thoughts to manage their emotions.
>
> —Jonice Webb (2014)

While we are busy trying to help children acknowledge and express their emotions, in point of fact most of us do not understand much about the complexity of emotions for ourselves. As children, we were taught to suppress feelings that were uncomfortable for the adults in our lives to manage—especially anger or sadness. Instead of learning to hold still and confront difficult emotions head on, adults taught us to ignore them, or worse still, push them aside as if they never happened, telling us those types of feelings were not nice, or that they were bad to have in the first place (Jacobson 2008). Most of us really do not know how to deal with our own feelings—let alone those of the children in our care.

In fact, as brain development neuroscientists have discovered, human emotions originate in the limbic system of the brain (Webb 2014). This is located below the cerebral cortex, the area of the brain where our cognitive thoughts originate. "In this way, our feelings are more a basic part of who we are than are our thoughts." Jonice Webb explains that our feelings are a "physiological part of our bodies, like fingernails or knees. Our emotions cannot be erased and will not be denied any more than we can erase or deny hunger or thirst" (121). So, according to Webb, many people who have been emotionally neglected consider emotions a burden. I know I did. In fact, I denied myself and buried important feelings to survive as a child. For if I showed anger for self-protection, it was greeted with enormous and dangerous (to a child) wrath from my mother. Not only did I consider emotions a burden, but, indeed, I denied I had them at all.

While most of us know that young children need our attention, there still seems to be a pervasive negative feeling about how children go about seeking it. In fact, over and over again, I get the distinct impression that children are considered disruptive, problematic, or just badly behaved whenever they seek out our attention. Somehow, adults still believe that children should be seen and not heard. Wherever I go, on planes, in stores or restaurants, or even in parks, I hear parents of young children apologizing for their children's noisiness. It is as if the sound of children's voices will be painful for adults to hear. Are we just too tired to relate to children when they are out in public? Keeping quiet and out of the way seem to be desired characteristics. Where did we learn this?

I remember as a child I tried to be invisible and not make too much noise around the adults in my home. Partly, I did this because my mother did not want me to disturb her husband, my stepfather. She subscribed to the old-school belief system that children should be seen and not heard, and they should especially not bother the men, who had been hard at work all day. If I sought out any kind of attention, the results were often disastrous. At the very least, I would be teased about how noisy I was. At the worst, I would be shamed for causing trouble for everyone. In the next chapter, I will suggest ideas for balancing children's need for attention with getting things done in the classroom community. However, right now, I would like us to consider where and how we developed our ideas and feelings about our own need for attention.

When We Face Ourselves

One thing I am sure of: we all need attention. Especially when we are children, as I have discussed at length in prior chapters, but also when we are adults. When I was director of a child care center, all the staff needed my attention, including teachers, caregivers, bookkeepers, receptionists, administrative assistants, cooks, and janitors. It took me awhile to understand this, and at first I was not very good at giving the kinds of feedback that made people feel important or worthwhile. But by the time I left the center to relocate to a different city eleven years later, I had learned that all of us adults were just like the children in our care. Everyone needed to be noticed and related to and made to feel worthwhile.

When teachers, administrators, and teacher educators ask me how to deal with children who seem to need constant attention, I first must ask, "How were you related to, or how did you acquire, seek out, and receive attention when you were a child?" For me to understand my own basic belief system about children needing attention, I must first closely examine the ways in which I was related to or ignored when I was a child, and how that affects my feelings today as an adult. Awareness does not always arrive like an epiphany or revelation, although it sometimes can. We might be doing, saying, or experiencing a situation when suddenly something clicks into place and we have an understanding of why we reacted the way we did, even making explicit connections with our own early childhood experiences.

More often than not, though, acquiring this awareness is hard work day to day, moment to moment. It takes a certain kind of training of our minds. We develop skills to look out for signs. For example, we may find it hardest to become aware when situations or relationships are challenging and we become lost in the passions of an emotionally charged moment. But we can always sit back quietly and reflect after the fact. We can analyze and make connections between that specific child, situation, or interaction and our feelings. Asking ourselves how we feel, how those feelings relate to the reality of the moment, and how the incident pushed some emotional buttons that trace back to things that happened to us when we were very young is one of the skills we can learn to help ourselves become aware of what we do in emotional situations. We can write our thoughts down to read later when we are calmer. Or we can just sit and think about it, holding still and allowing ourselves to really feel the emotions that rise up for us in those emotionally charged situations with young children in our care.

Out of all the education literature that I reviewed as I was writing this book, including books and articles about discipline, few talked about how teachers' emotional development affects or influences interactions with children. I became excited when I found a couple of sentences acknowledging that the teacher could set an emotional tone in the classroom, even though it went no deeper than that: "Every morning, Ms. Mitchell thinks about how her feelings will affect her teaching. If she feels frustrated or overwhelmed when she arrives at school, she takes a deep breath and makes a plan for managing her emotions so that she can fully engage with her students and coteachers" (Tominey et al. 2017, 6).

In Enid Elliot's important book *We're Not Robots: The Voices of Daycare Providers* (2007), she explains that not all early childhood educators are prepared for the "complicated work of caregiving."

She worked with the staff of her school-based program to help them reflect about what attachment meant to them personally by have them write notes informally to each other in a journal, which staff could take home or write in during their lunch breaks. One of the staff, "Jade," wrote in the journal:

> I'm finding reading and talking about others' views on attachment and detachment extremely helpful. I realize it is not as simple as the isolated incidents of caregiving in this center. We all come with our own attachment behaviors of our past! You feel so deeply and then begin to question just what is healthy or not in these feelings. Letting the child take the lead seems to me to be the key for judging healthy relationships. This calls for a constant awareness from us, the adults in the situation. Not always easy, but then growth and awareness aren't always an easy path. . . . I feel that the thin line between healthy and unhealthy is becoming clearer as we all work to define it.

For us to make connections between the personal, emotional experiences of our own childhood and our interactions and behaviors with children, we need to know our story about how we became who we are (Jacobson 2008).

In both of my previous books (2003, 2008), I describe how I was affected by how I was disciplined as a child. Leading up to the writing of this book, I did a lot of self-work, alone and with a therapist, to understand how I developed my beliefs and ideas about children needing our attention. This work became especially challenging for me recently, as I have discussed, when my mother died one week short of her hundredth birthday, for I found myself experiencing emotions that had been stifled since childhood. Somehow, with her passing, I have been able to release some of these feelings. Lo and behold, they pertain to the topic of this book; namely, how much I longed for my mother's attention growing up, and how it eluded me for all the reasons I will describe here.

Indeed, following my mother's death, I found myself experiencing several months of what seemed like uncontrollable feelings of longing—longing for the emotional mothering that I never had growing up. Waves of longing washed over me day in and day out, and I found myself weeping constantly whatever I did and wherever I went: driving to the grocery store, mowing the lawn, walking in the woods, sitting on my porch drinking tea, gardening, cooking, and especially while writing this book. I began to understand about how so many of the choices I had made as a young woman had to do with that very longing I was now, finally, allowing myself to feel. My therapist suggested that I was at last allowing myself to experience what I felt as a child but had repressed to survive. One of the things I discovered with this new awakening is that I became an expert in self-regulation very early on. In other words, when I was a child and had no one to whom I could turn to get my emotional needs met, I quickly learned to numb out emotions and get on with life and not to "bother" people by asking for help.

Understanding and processing the details of my story also help me forgive my parents for the pain they caused me, for much of what happened was due to the timing of my birth as well as the circumstances surrounding those times. I was born in Zimbabwe, which in 1949 was known as Southern Rhodesia, a British colony. I was born the year after the state of Israel was established. The story that I was told growing up was that my father wanted to name me Dolores. He came from the Greek island of Rhodes and spoke Ladino, a mixture of classical Spanish and Yiddish. My mother did not want to call me a name that means "sorrow," so they chose the Hebrew name of Tamar in honor of the newly established state of Israel.

I was born quickly and easily, so I was told. The joke was that I was eager to get out of there! I was the fourth of my mother's children, and the fourth of my father's, as both had been married prior to their short-lived marriage of five years. My half siblings were all much older than me, ranging from twenty years old to six. My father was fifty-five when I was born, my mother thirty-two.

During the short time my father and mother were married, my mother had an affair with her soon-to-be third husband. I know this because she told me. She also described to me that when she discovered she was pregnant with me, she went to her lover and said, "What am I going to do? I am having his [my father's] child." I heard that story many times, although I cannot remember how young I was when I first heard it. Needless to say, it did not make me feel particularly wanted.

In My Father's House

When I was four years old, my mother and father divorced. I would visit my father every second weekend in his home. Sometimes I visited him in his upholstery shop in town. I remember that he was pleased to see me when I walked into his shop. When I started learning French in high school, my father sent me my first French dictionary. He bought me my first piano when I was a teenager, paid my way to Israel when I emigrated to that country at nineteen, sent money for my wedding a few years later, and bought me my first stove. My mother repeatedly told me that my father was stingy with money, and she would share her anxiety with me whenever she asked him to buy things for me. She could not pay for things for me herself, she would say, because the money in our family belonged to her third husband. I did not experience my father as stingy. He gave me a weekly allowance, was gentle with me like a grandfather, and seemed proud to show me off to his friends.

My father remarried his first wife after he divorced my mother. My stepmother came to Africa from Alexandria, Egypt. They had had three children before their divorce and my father's brief interlude with my mother. Their first daughter, Clara, died from pneumonia when she was seven. My stepmother would bathe me as soon as I arrived for a weekend visit. She claimed that I wasn't clean enough coming from my mother's house. She would take me from the front door, put me in a bath, and make me scrub my knees in particular. Once when I was young, perhaps six years old or so, she put me outside on the front porch because I cried for my mother. I sat alone and frightened out in the darkening evening and never cried to go home again. My father and stepmother slept in different bedrooms. When I stayed over for the weekend, I slept in my father's room, which had two beds, in the bed next to his.

By then my father was in his sixties. He had a chamber pot under his bed. During the night, I would wake up to hear him urinating in that pot. I would lie quietly, keeping very still so that he would not think I was awake. I felt afraid and uncomfortable. After I turned ten, my father never took me home to his house for visits again. He would only take me out on short outings: walks in the park, movies, or drives out in the country for tea. Sometimes he would take me to visit his friends. I would sit and watch them as they played *shesh-besh* (backgammon) or drank tea and talked about politics. I remember my father expressing pride about me. He spoke many languages, including Ladino, English, French, Spanish, and some Russian. He was gentle and loving, and only once in my teenage years did he admonish me for something he did not approve of. His scolding was as gentle as could be, and I learned from it quickly, not wanting to disappoint him. I do not know why my stepmother would not allow me in their home. I always thought it was because I no longer reminded her of their first daughter, Clara, who had died of pneumonia when she was seven. I seem to remember my father or someone telling me that as long as I had reminded my stepmother of Clara, she allowed me in her house.

Thinking back, in a way my stepmother paid more attention to me than my mother did. Even though she insisted I must not have been cleaned properly in my mother's house, she took the trouble to bathe me—and to make sure I scrubbed my knees. At home with my mother, no one took the time to look in on me even in a negative sense. In addition, my stepmother would sometimes take me with her to town to a department store, Haddon and Sly, for tea and *millefeuilles*, a French cake made with "thousands" of layers of flaky pastry, filled with a sweet custard pudding and powdered sugar sprinkled generously on the top—much like what Italians call a Napoleon. I used to love that outing with her. She would dress me up prettily, and I behaved very well. I would sit still watching her as she dyed her gray hair blue, taking great care to roll it up tight with large hair pins, and also as she put on makeup. She wore white gloves as she drove us into downtown Bulawayo.

My stepmother held her cigarette in a cigarette holder when she smoked. I used to watch her, wishing that one day I might look as sophisticated and beautiful as she was. I longed for her to like me but always felt too dirty, ugly, clumsy, and in the way. My father seemed afraid of her and gently warned me to behave well so as not to make her angry. I had to call her Aunty Rose. Once, I called her Rose, and she became furious, shouting and yelling at me and my father. I sat on my father's lap and wept quietly with fear. He took me home early that day. I learned to call her Aunty Rose from then on. Rose bred parakeets. Her favorite, Jackie Boy, sat on her shoulder and pecked gently at her tongue, which she turned toward him, thrusting out chewed almonds. She had a locked closet full of candy, which she would give me if I was good. Rose explained to me that she hired only black African servants whose palms were light colored. She believed that they were cleaner than others.

My father died when I was thirty-three. He was eighty-eight. I returned to Zimbabwe to spend the last four days of his life with him and was by his side in the hospital room when he died. I was unable to cry. I did not realize how much I loved my father, nor how much he loved me, until he died, because I feared being disloyal to my mother, who openly disliked him and told me so unendingly when I was growing up.

I find it harder to write about my memories of childhood with my mother. When I reflect back, it mostly feels like a dark, lonely, and fearful period of my life, which I spent either worrying about my mother's emotional well-being or fearing her wrath if I thought, felt, or, worse still, expressed what I experienced or needed. I grew up anxious and worried about being a burden to my mother and stepfather.

My Mother and Me

My birth in my mother's family was sandwiched between my mother's favorites, my two brothers, each from different fathers: the first, six years older than me from a father my mother admired, and the second, eight years younger than me, from a father my mother loved passionately. I suppose you could say it was bad luck for me that I was the progeny of my father, who came in between my mother's two other husbands, and who was openly despised and ridiculed by her and my stepfather all the years that I grew up.

Two incidents, decades apart, have stood out for me in my memory as I have tried to understand my emotional story. I allow myself to experience old, stifled feelings and realize that both incidents have remained vivid in my brain because they represent clearly for me the essence of my relationship with my mother. The first incident I wrote about at the end of chapter 3, when my mother beat me and flung me around the room one night when I was ill. As I look back and reflect on that incident, I think it was the night I officially lost my emotional birthright. The way I understand it, from that night, I was no longer a priority for her.

The second incident happened more than a decade ago when as a grown woman, I traveled to Israel, as I did each year to visit my mother, who was then in her late eighties. At that time, she was living in a small cottage on her estate, having rented out her larger house. By then I knew that she planned to leave her entire estate with all its contents to my younger brother, for she had notified us all of her decision over twenty years prior, before I emigrated to the United States. During that summer of my visit, my mother's cottage was unbearably hot, and she had to haul her laundry to the top of her property to my brother's cottage. I surprised her by purchasing a small washing machine, an air-conditioning unit, and a CD player so that she could listen to the classical music she loved.

One day, shortly after I had given her those gifts, my mother said, "Tamar, choose an ornament to take back to America with you, because as you know, everything is being left to your brother when I die." I was surprised at her offer, and although she did not mention it, I assumed it was her way of showing gratitude for the items I had bought for her. I looked around the room until my eyes rested on a porcelain figurine of the princess and the frog. Even though the crown on the little frog seated at the princess's feet was a little chipped, I loved the ornament, which had been in our home since I was young. Feeling excited for the chance to receive such a gift from my mother, I told her of my choice. "No," she responded sharply and instantly, "That's your brother's favorite." As I was familiar with her usual double-bind interactions with me, I regrouped quickly, giggled, and said, "You choose something for me then." I cannot remember exactly what she chose for me, but when I returned to my home in the United States, I threw it away.

At the time, I don't remember feeling much of anything about that incident, and for years when I retold that story, I described it as a humorous anecdote, some kind of idiosyncratic event about my mother's outrageousness. Recently, since my mother's death, I finally allowed myself to feel how that incident had, in fact, hurt me. After all, she had bequeathed her entire estate, including furnishings, artworks, and property to my brother, and she had put me in the position of a double bind: choosing any item, which she immediately took back. In addition, I had just given her items necessary for her comfort. And yet she chose to deny me in that manner.

While writing this book and reflecting on my relationship with my mother, I suddenly understood how unkindly my mother acted toward me. It hurt me deeply, and I wept, realizing that this incident had stayed with me for more than a decade because it was representative of how she had always treated me: like an outsider with no rights. When I was eight years old and ill with a tapeworm during that night I described earlier, she beat me and yelled at me thunderously, all the while voicing how I was a disturbance and burden to her husband and new baby. I had to forfeit a mother's love and support in times of physical need for others more important to her. And then again, years later when choosing any ornament at her bidding, I forfeited my wishes for someone more important to her.

In my older age, I understand what a difficult childhood my mother had herself and realize that for most of my childhood and into my adolescence, she was probably worried about losing my stepfather. In addition, I think she just wanted to start over and have a new little family of three, and there I was, a small child from a man she hated—in the way. In point of fact, to this day I do not know if my stepfather actually was concerned about how much I ate or how much noise I made. However, this was the lesson I learned in my early childhood: not to be a burden on anyone. And definitely not to express any feelings that would make my mother more anxious than she already was. For me, it was not only that I did not receive the unconditional love and attention a small child deserves, it was that I learned to constantly *give* my mother the love and attention *she* needed, thereby forfeiting my own emotional needs.

After writing this passage, I went to my computer and searched for a picture of a small statue depicting the princess and the frog. I discovered on a website an original Rosenthal porcelain figurine from 1939, an almost exact replica of the one my mother had denied me in the choice she offered me so many years ago. It was costly, but I instantly purchased it as a gift for the emotionally deprived child within me. When the figurine arrived in the mail, carefully wrapped in a large box, I lifted it out and wept. I placed the princess and the frog on my desk in front of me as I continued to write this book. I figured that it is never too late to heal the deprived child within me, and for me to give *me* the love and attention I lacked growing up.

Even though I have touched on only a couple of incidents that helped develop my worldview with regard to children needing attention, I hope my doing so encourages you, the reader, to contemplate the important details that stand out for you about your own childhood emotional story. Getting in touch with what makes us tick emotionally and making connections between our childhood story and interactions with children help us become more intentional in our behaviors—especially in emotional situations. Needing attention and most disciplinary situations are emotional situations!

Adults Are Not Bad Just Because They Can't Always Provide Attention

If we can accept that we need and want attention, perhaps we can make a bridge to understanding and accepting that when children need our attention, they are not bad or disruptive—even if we can't always provide it. I think that as early childhood educators, we feel guilty when we are unable to provide the attention that we know children need. But here's the thing: we are not bad if we cannot always provide it! We have only two hands and one body and usually way too many children in one classroom for us to reach every one of them when they most need it. In addition, we are not always aware when they most need it because our judgment of situations is so often fraught with our own anxieties, memories, and unmet needs. Elliot (2007) reminds us that "caregivers are affected emotionally by their work with [children] and families; they are also involved in a process of emotional growth" (49).

Therefore, it is essential that as teachers of young children, we become aware of how we developed emotionally when we were young, and constantly negotiate the personal with the professional in our relationships with children. This is not a onetime self-help suggestion. This process is ongoing for most of our lives, once we get the hang of it. It is a skill that is worth having because it helps us understand why we do what we do. This is important for becoming a professional. We learn that what we do and how we interact or behave matter. This knowledge has an effect on children's emotional development and enhances our own relationships.

Researching the Self

In this chapter, I have described in detail chosen sections of my life story and emotional script as I know it. It has taken me years to remember, fine-tune, and analyze how I came to be who I am today, specifically as it relates to my attitudes, beliefs, and ideas about why and how children need our attention. In researching myself, I have used various tools: analysis with a therapist, writing in journals and on a blog, and interviewing half siblings and old friends who knew what was happening in our family when I was too young to remember. I discovered from them that the short four or five years my father and mother were together were tumultuous and noisy with lots of fighting. They were terribly unsuited for each other, my father twenty years older than my mother and rebounding from a difficult divorce. And who knows what my mother saw in my father—security, perhaps? Their marriage was a mistake, and giving birth to their only daughter, me, was probably a mistake too. After listening to one of the stories my half brother from my father's side told me, I remembered vividly when I was very small—perhaps four or five years old—sitting on my parents' bed while they were shouting at each other over my head.

Exploring the journey of how I came to be me, I have concluded that my interactions and behaviors with others are affected by how I was treated. If we interact with children based *only* on our intuition, how our emotional buttons are pressed, or from our gut, we can unintentionally create situations that replicate some of the pain we endured as children. However, when we examine closely how each emotionally loaded situation with young children taps into our own childhood experiences, we are able to stop and change the way we think about things. We do not always have to do to others what was done to us. We have a choice. As professionals, we can decide to do what is developmentally appropriate for children emotionally, physically, and cognitively. However, we don't have a choice when we are clouded or burdened by unresolved childhood issues.

When I look back on many of the events and interactions in my childhood, I notice that I developed a sense that I was unwanted, a burden to my mother and father as they tried to live their lives with other spouses and children. I sought out their attention by being invisible, serving their emotional needs before mine, and hoping all the while to be noticed for my goodness. Since I am only human, however, I still had emotional needs and feelings, and from time to time they would bubble up and out. When that would happen, the reaction from my mother was always the same. Either through yelling, screaming, or crying, she would tell me that what I was experiencing was a lie, a performance to "destroy" her—all terrifying for a young child who egocentrically believes she is to blame or responsible for everything. Or my mother would become tight-lipped and would withdraw affection in a way that made me weep and plead to know what I had done wrong, apologizing for things I had not done—just as terrifying for a young child. Young children are always scared of losing their parents' affection, fearing they won't survive without it.

These childhood realities became the foundation for my emotional life script, and I took them with me into my adult years. Starting at twenty-one, I strove tirelessly to compensate emotionally for every single child or adult who crossed my path. In other words, I tried to give everyone what I wished had been given to me. While this made me generous and respectful of other people's feelings on the one hand, on the other it biased me to err on the side of kindness and compassion when sometimes tough love was needed. And, of course, it came at a high price for me, for I constantly put aside my needs and desires to ensure the other person's emotional wishes.

How Did I Come to Know MySelf over All These Years?

First, I held out hope and accepted the kindness and support of strangers along the way. I taught myself how to reach out to people who I sensed would provide me the type of support I needed—usually people who would listen to me and validate my experience. Compassion, respect, and nonjudgmental characteristics were important to me. I learned that they were important for my relationships with children and also for healing myself along the way. Second, I learned to express myself through writing. At first, I wrote journals when emotions seemed too uncomfortable to bear. After that, I started to write blogs, which were an excellent way of receiving feedback from people. So, not only was I able to express myself, but with blogging I could practice and improve my writing style. Third, I took myself to therapy. Processing and talking through my life story was important for me to learn a different reality about myself. In my previous book (2008), I called that "changing my emotional script."

Self-Reflection Is Critical for Emotional Development

In both my previous books (2003, 2008), I wrote extensively about the importance of reflective practice, and, indeed, most early childhood professionals understand the importance of knowing why we do what we do. When we reflect on our practice, we are able to understand the basis for the decisions we make. We become more intentional based on knowledge of child development, our life experiences, and our understanding of best practices. The same is true for our emotional development and our understanding of children's emotions. Learning about how we tick emotionally helps us refine our interactions with children and prevents our own past emotional experiences from getting in the way or clouding our perception of what is happening for the child in our care. We can learn to detach from our own past baggage and the emotional noise in our minds, and clearly listen and connect to children in the moment.

I delve deeply into my childhood to get to the bottom of it all in my search to understand myself. That has worked for me. It feels like reading a good detective story—mysterious and revealing. To be sure, sometimes it can be painful because confronting our discomfort is never easy. But there are moments of epiphany and revelation that excite and amaze me, as well as provide me with different choices in how to feel and behave. In addition, doing the hard work of self-research, reflection, self-understanding, and self-alteration takes time and enables me to access those feelings that were repressed so long ago. This is a challenge because accessing and acknowledging those feelings can be frightening and may seem dangerous even to contemplate. After all, that's why they were stifled in the first place.

This process does not work for everyone. Each person has their own way of working through or learning about their past emotional history. Through reading, taking courses, painting, drawing, or keeping a journal, or sometimes just talking with a good friend or colleague, we learn a lot about ourselves. If we choose to work with children in any capacity, I believe we have an obligation to do some type of self-work as it pertains to understanding our early childhood. For we know that we lay the foundation for brain development in the earliest years, ages birth through five, especially for emotional memory and attachment. We know that we transfer what we learned about attachment and relationships onto our future interactions with others. Most of us repeat negative or positive patterns of behavior we learned as children almost as if we have been given some kind of an emotional script for life. We have the power within us to change those patterns and rewrite the script when it becomes no longer useful for our survival as adults.

We have an obligation to become professional and intentional and understand why we do what we do. We do this so that we can interact and behave in the best possible ways to enhance children's emotional and social development. That is, of course, if we, as early childhood educators, take our work seriously and genuinely care about children and families.

Chapter 5

Relationships, Relationships, Relationships!

Respect is key to relationships. When you show consideration for another person you communicate to them that they are valued. Feeling valued contributes to a sense of trust and self-esteem and is reflected in the individual's ability to form and maintain relationships with others.
—Toni Christie (2011)

EARLY MORNING. Still dark even though the clock reads 6:00 a.m. I look away from the computer and stretch widely in my chair, my arms reaching upward and my feet extending out into the room. Two cats sit still and quiet—sphinxes in the early morning. Patient and waiting. As I stretch and sigh, they look up slowly from their posts—Mimi on the carpet close by and Oscar on his stand, huddled down. I realize how dependent they are on me. They await their breakfast, and I am the only one who will give it to them at this time of the day. I realize that they need me for affection, encouragement, discipline, and food. Much like any young child.

My thoughts stray to when I was a child, and I remember sitting very still, silently watching the adults around me. Keeping track of their movements and facial expressions, and listening for intonations as they spoke, all the while gleaning information that was important for my emotional and physical survival. A shift in my mother's face, a slight shadow, tightening lips, softening or glaring eyes, clenching of her jaw—these were some of the signs that taught me to relax around her or become afraid, wary of what I did or said. As a child still learning about a new environment and getting to know new people in my life, I trod with caution and took seriously things that were said in anger, or even with humor. Sarcasm was confusing and hurtful, because as a young child, learning to survive could be treacherous and lonely or safe and warm depending on the reactions and behaviors of the significant adults in my life.

As adults, how often we forget that children are sitting or standing silently by, watching our every move or unintentional wince, making assumptions and interpretations, finding meaning that is relevant to their unique and egoistic perspective. Moment by moment they drink in our everyday reactions and behaviors, learning about their worth as future adults. How helpful it would be for children if only we could talk them through what they may be understanding about how we are feeling. But, then again, do we always know what we are feeling when we are around children?

If you have made it through the book to this chapter, I hope you agree with me that the children in our care desperately need our attention. I hope you are on your way to learning all the ways you received attention or were ignored when you were a child, and how that affected your perception of children needing your attention now. And with all that knowledge and understanding, perhaps you are thinking, as so many attendees at my workshops do: "Okay, okay, I know this! But what do I *do* now?"

In this chapter, I will offer some thoughts and strategies that have worked for me over the years. Sometimes all the developmental knowledge in the world does nothing for us in intensely emotional situations. Rather, our emotional memories of punishments rise up and cloud what we know to be important about discipline (Jacobson 2008). Our early childhood emotional memories can be powerful, for it is through what we experienced with our parents and guardians, who were so important to our very existence, that we learned to survive.

In 2006, as a member of the Delaware Valley Association for the Education of Young Children conference committee, I hosted Bruce Perry, who was the keynote speaker at the annual conference in Philadelphia. After Perry's three-hour keynote presentation to an audience of over a thousand people, a young woman rushed into the hall directly up to us at the head table. While puffing and panting, she spluttered, "Can you tell me what I missed? I need to report on this presentation at work, but I didn't make it in time to hear it." I responded to the woman, "What? You want Dr. Perry to sum up a three-hour presentation in one sentence?" She nodded her head in the affirmative. So I turned toward Perry in disbelief, not knowing what more to say. He smiled at me and said, "Tamar, tell her it's about *relationships, relationships, relationships*."

Indeed, J. Ronald Lally and Peter Mangione concur:

> The foundation of brain development is social and emotional development grounded in caring relationships. If caregivers are mindful of how a child's whole experience—particularly the emotional tenor—influences the developing brain, they can provide caring relationships that help the child feel secure and open up to an engaging world of exploration and learning throughout the early years. (Lally and Mangione 2017, 23)

One of the key ingredients for cultivating authentic and meaningful relationships is having the capacity for empathy. Empathy lets us put ourselves in another person's shoes and imagine how they may be feeling. When a child is anxious or stressed, we will be able to stop, observe, wonder what he is feeling, and then relate to him by trying out different strategies or discussions without ignoring or becoming punitive.

Perry stresses that early childhood is a critical period for developing empathy and that it is "shaped every day by what we do and what we don't do":

> Consequently, while we are born for love, we need to receive it in certain, specific ways early in life to benefit most from its mercy. We need to practice love as we grow through different social experiences to best be able to give it back in abundance. The brain becomes what it does most frequently . . . if we don't practice empathy, we can't become more empathetic. If we don't interact with people, we can't improve our connections to them. If we don't ease another's stress through caring contact, we will all be increasingly distressed. (Szalavitz and Perry 2010, 289)

It is the day-to-day doing and practicing of empathy in our relationships with young children that model for them our humanity. They won't learn this from a unit on sharing and caring as much as from what they observe in our daily personal behaviors toward them, their parents and guardians, and colleagues and coworkers. Empathic connection and relationship are more about being present and bearing witness than about giving advice or trying to fix things, writes Shefali Tsabary (2010). It is about becoming conscious while being present, and developing skills like listening and observing children's bodies and gestures:

> Why do we feel we must constantly advise our children, always impart some gem of wisdom, give our opinion on everything? I suggest the reason lies in ourselves, not in what our children require. . . . Engaged presence involves being a witness to [children's] experiences, allowing them to sit in what they are feeling without any insinuation that they need to move beyond this state. . . . We are talking about empathy [which

> allows] the individual to experience . . . in their own way, with us bearing witness. (Tsabary 2010, 195–98)

In this chapter, I provide some guidelines that lie at the core of developing relationships and giving children the attention they need and want.

Remembering That One Size Does Not Fit All

The first thing to think about in how we choose strategies about giving, receiving, and withholding attention is how we understand it ourselves. It is my negotiation with self that helps me decide how to proceed: allowing myself to access emotional memories of empathic relationships, of feelings attached to those memories, of what presses my emotional buttons, and so on.

When it comes to the strategies to choose when children need our attention, one size doesn't fit all. Each child is unique. This might sound like a cliché, but it is truer than you think, or remember, when faced with a group of two-, three-, or four-year-olds. Not only are we all unique, but our parents, guardians, cultures, family configurations, childhood physical and emotional environments, birth order, personalities, learning styles, perceptions—all are unique too. Therefore, whether you choose a "good job," a pat on the head and a cookie, or social isolation in time-out, these strategies are not going to work for every child in the same way. And by the way, the same goes for us as adults. We are unique individuals, every one of us, just like the children in our care. In our relationships with one another as adults, there is not one size that fits us all either. Lilian Katz reminds us of complex factors that contribute to the kinds of interactions teachers have with young children:

> Many young children are shy in the presence of adults who are new to them, or are not accustomed to extended

> conversations with adults, and it often takes time for them to get used to interacting with those who are not members of their family or their familiar neighborhood, or their own cultural or ethnic group. Helping young children requires great skill, social as well as intellectual, on the part of the teacher. (Katz 2009, 9)

Katz goes on to suggest that as teachers we should "cultivate our own intellects and nourish the mind," and that is as important as cultivating "our capacities for understanding, compassion, and caring."

Giving or withholding attention has everything to do with the types of relationships we develop with every child in our care. And because each child is unique, the way we develop these relationships will be specific to each child. Children who have received a lot of quality attention since they were born are more trusting and have faith that we will come through and mean what we say when we call out, "Be there in a minute!" Those who have been disappointed or left to self-soothe for hours on end through stressful crying alone in a crib may not believe us as easily (Wright Glenn 2015). This seems like common sense, but I am aware that many people do not agree with me. They believe that a system of punishments and rewards is much more effective when teaching children to self-regulate. In addition, others claim that there simply isn't time to spend developing relationships with every child. Teachers are short-handed and have many children to relate to. Someone is surely going to get left out, and what about all the paperwork that needs to be completed, like observations, data input, progress reports, and lesson plans?

According to Dombro, Jablon, and Stetson (2011), we can turn an "everyday interaction into a powerful interaction" (6–7). We do this with just three steps:

- The first step is simply being present, meaning that we are intentional, aware, and in the moment—ready and open to engage with a child.

- The second step requires that we "connect" with children. Here the authors explain that connection comes when you "acknowledge and validate children by letting them know you see them, are interested in them, and want to spend time with them. Connecting in this way awakens the sense of trust and security that previous positive interactions between you and the child are helping to develop. As your relationships with children grow deeper, children feel more confident and focused, and they are more open to learning from you."
- After being present and connecting in this manner, we are then able to carry out the third step: extending children's learning with open-ended questions and discussion. What is important in this process is the connection—the relationships we develop with the children we are trying to care for and educate. To facilitate children's learning, we need to relate to them.

Understanding Our Worldview

Here is where your worldview takes hold. Do you believe that the world is a harsh and cruel place and that you must prepare young children for hard times ahead with tough punishments and consequential stickers? Or do you believe that children are complex, whole human beings who deserve our full attention, empathy, and compassion? These different worldviews affect the steps you choose to take and the methods and strategies you will use with young children who are demanding your attention at appropriate or inappropriate moments. I remember when my son was eighteen months old and a friend would visit for tea in the afternoon. As we started to chatter away as friends are wont to do, he would climb on my lap, hold my face with both his hands, and pull me around to look *only* at him. My friend would become quite agitated and make snide remarks to show me that I needed to limit his behavior. I would look directly at my son, smile at him, and hug him, telling him that I loved him always and only. Then, after a little while, he would climb off my lap and toddle off to play.

Now, granted, I was alone at home with only him. I would probably handle it differently if I had a group of eight to ten toddlers, all struggling to climb into my lap for my attention. But, honestly, not that differently. Because if I am aware that this is an egocentric stage and that each child is unique with different needs and capabilities, I would have to find ways to reach every one. Exhausting? Yes! But I figure that I chose this profession intentionally because I want to give children the option of understanding the world through compassionate discipline rather than shaming and exclusion. Therefore, it is my responsibility to find ways to reach every child. Part of the wonder and magic of working with young children is being able to discover all the different ways to relate to everyone. I still remember thirty years later how my stepdaughter, the daughter of my second husband, age seven or eight at the time, once exclaimed, "I love being sick at Tamar's!" She was referring to my covering her with a blanket, giving her soup, tea, and treats, and spoiling her rotten.

Considering Discipline Strategies

> When we think of discipline and young children, most of us filter our knowledge of child development and appropriate practice through our own early childhood experiences and [emotional] memories of punishments received or witnessed. That is why, when I ask adults to share ways they were disciplined, they usually reply with a list of punishments. . . . We become confused between punishment—"Sit in the corner facing the wall until you can be good!"—and discipline—"In our class, I want everyone to be safe here. When you threaten

> someone with throwing a block at them, no one is safe."
>
> —Tamar Jacobson (2008)

I go into some detail with a number of strategies for disciplining children in my book *"Don't Get So Upset!"* (2008). I like to say that what works for me may not always work for you. First, these suggestions are based on strategies I tried out over the course of many years. I experimented with many different ideas. If something did not work at first, I tried something else. I did not give up. Somehow, I had faith that eventually something must work. I was inclined to look for solutions that involved firm limits without punishments. I was willing to hold children, put them on my back—anything—so that they would not feel rejected. I was able to be firm when there was a question of anyone's safety, but this took time, experience, and practice.

The ideas I wrote about in my last book include making wise curriculum choices, giving relevant consequences, and using a punching cushion. These ideas still hold true for me today, so I won't repeat them here, but rather refer you to them (see Jacobson 2008). However, allow me to mention a few more as a reminder and then add one additional idea about time-out for teachers:

- **Carry children on your back.** This was something I learned as a young child growing up in Africa, having been carried on my nanny's back. I still recommend this strategy for teachers of young children, even though I recognize that some people will not choose to use this. I wrote:

  > The proximity to my body was immediately soothing and I still had my hands free to work with the other children who needed me. Second, if there was a child who was biting the other children, the perfect place for her was on my back. That way, I knew where she was and could help her stop the behavior in a firm but loving way. . . . Each time I scooped up a child onto my back. I would say something like, "I want everyone to be safe here. Come and be with me until you are safe again

and can stop biting . . . punching . . . hitting . . . running away . . . etc." (Jacobson 2008, 134–35)

- **Choose your battles.** There are so many things to negotiate with children when their behaviors challenge us. Therefore, in your negotiation with yourself about which battles to choose, ask yourself these questions: "What is your bottom line? Which behaviors can you tolerate more than others? . . . How would you identify what is important for you with regard to [their] behaviors and manners?" (Jacobson 2008, 137).
- **Follow through immediately and mean what you say.** Be immediate and explicit, firm and clear with what you want the child to do, especially when you want to prevent dangerous situations. If you really mean it, you will go directly over to the child, kneel down low so that you are face-to-face with the young child, and gently but firmly express what is on your mind. You don't have to shout or yell for a child to understand that you are serious about something.

Time-Out for Teachers

Here's another strategy that I think works well in certain situations. When your work with children becomes too much to deal with and you are feeling overwhelmed, take a few minutes for a personal time-out. You don't have to go far away, nor do you have to be away for long. Tell your coteacher, assistant, or supervisor that you need a few minutes to breathe, and step away from the action. As you pull back and even before you head out for a drink of water, think this thought: "If I were a child in my program, how would I like to be treated?" Take a moment to think about this. Whenever I pose this question at workshops or in presentations, participants and attendees immediately come up with many different answers. Probably you will too. They say things like, "If I were a child in my program, I would like to be treated with respect, love, kindness, empathy, and so forth," and "I would like to feel safe, validated, listened to, and so on." At this point, I invite you to feel free to add additional answers that are specific to your needs. Think back to when you were a child and remember a favorite adult who treated you in these ways that you describe. Can you picture her face, the sound of her voice, or even the touch of her hands? Bring those memories front and center as you breathe deeply before you reenter the classroom.

I guarantee you that as you return to the fray, your attitude will have shifted. Instead of shouting, becoming punitive or even harsh, something will change within you. You may be able to see the child you were locked in battle with a few minutes earlier in a different light. This, my friends, is empathy. At that point, you will be able to choose those strategies that make sense for you and that child in the moment. Your choice will be intentional, based on knowledge of child development as well as an awareness of how you—and the child—may be feeling.

Bear in mind, though, that each person has a different experience with those ideas and feelings about how you would like to be treated in your program. For some, love was accompanied by beatings when the adult said things like, "This hurts me more than it hurts you—I beat you because I love and care about you." "Why are you crying? I'll give you something to cry about." These kinds of treatments can cause resentment and sometimes even feelings of revenge. But mostly, children submerge those feelings and forget about them until they pop up in contexts when we least expect them. Think about this: Where does all that resentment go? Where and how can children share feelings of anger, frustration, and resentment? More importantly for you right now as you reflect on this: What did *you* do as a child with those kinds of feelings? Who could you share them with? If they pop up from time to time, how do you manage those feelings? And how do they factor into the decisions you make about what strategies to use with this or that child who challenges you with his behaviors, with seeking too much or too little attention?

Designing the Physical Environment

The physical environment of your room also has an impact on relationships. Before beginning this topic, I invite you to take a seat on the floor of your classroom or home environment. Sit cross-legged, and look around the room you are in. You are now about the height of a three-year-old child. As you look around, notice all the things a young child might be able to see from their eye level. What do you see? What is missing? What is too high up for them to notice? Where might they choose to run and hide? For example, you might notice the tall legs of an adult table—an excellent spot for children to hide under. Put yourself in the mind of a child. If you were a child in your program, what would you like to see or discover in the environment—*at your eye level*?

Relating to children and paying attention to them are not only about how they feel. They are also about what children are thinking. In discussing the need for developing "standards of experience" about the types of experiences children should have "much" of the time, Lilian Katz says that children should "have experience of confidence in their intellectual powers. . . . Their ideas and suggestions are responded to with respect [even if they might not make sense at that moment]. . . . [They need] frequent experiences of being intellectually engaged" (Katz 2014, video). She reminds us that we should "cultivate the habit of speaking to children as if they are young people with minds . . . [and that] intellectual goals and their related activities address the life of the mind in its fullest sense, including a range of aesthetic and moral abilities" (Katz 2014).

The way we design the physical environment sets the stage for the development of aesthetic awareness and sensibilities and gives children (and their parents) an expectation of how to behave or what to do in the room. For example, if there is a wide-open space in a toddler room, chances are children will start to run back and forth. If, on the other hand, there are some small indoor climbers or structures, the toddlers will have to slow down and climb—something they adore doing—rather than just run around willy-nilly. Not that running around willy-nilly is a bad thing! It just might not be what you want them to do indoors in your classroom.

Every picture, poster, plant, birdcage, sofa, armchair, table, rug, cushion—any item that you choose to place in the environment—has a purpose and should be thought out intentionally just as you would plan for any curriculum or activity. What you choose to place in your classroom, or home, describes to children what they can or cannot do, what you believe about aesthetics in general, and how you value them as emotional, social, intellectual beings. For example, you can show them that you believe they are intelligent by giving them mind-expanding opportunities with pictures of real children and families, and prints from art galleries on the walls. Real armchairs or sofas, rugs, and cushions soften the environment and invite children to feel at home, rather than as if they are in a cold, harsh institution. When I was director of a campus child care center, I brought in plants of all sizes and colors, which hung from the ceiling near the windows and stood in large pots around the center and in the classrooms. There was also a cage with parakeets close to my office space. If children did not tend to the plants and animals, they observed the adults who did.

Creating an aesthetic environment is good for the adults as well. Sitting in an armchair with children snuggled in with you is a much better way to read a book together than sitting a distance away on a higher chair while the children sit up straight with legs crossed on tiny mats on a hard floor. Reading becomes associated with pleasure and loving attention in a large, soft armchair. Adults feel respected when they are surrounded by plants, artistic prints, and real photographs of real people and places. When we are surrounded by beauty, we can feel relaxed and inspired, and more importantly, we have space to think about what we are seeing.

On the other hand, you can choose to trivialize children by offering them only cartoon characters on the wall, which give very little opportunity for expanding their thinking, or put up so much unrelated stuff that there is no space to rest one's eyes. I have been in classrooms where it is impossible to notice what is on the walls because it is so crowded and jumbled: here a poster about washing hands, there a smiling giraffe that says it is good to read, here a calendar, there a weather chart, and on and on. Most classrooms have little space for children's work to be displayed, and often their work is displayed chaotically without providing context for how they created it.

In our child care center, we had a large linoleum floor area for the younger and older toddlers to eat lunch and snack. They sat together at small, round tables with an adult. There were child-sized pitchers of milk or water for the children to choose and pour for themselves. Food was placed in the center of the table, and the children were invited to serve themselves. At the end of the meal, they would toddle off to a different table to bus their plates and cups. Often they would spill liquids or food as they learned how to pour and serve themselves. Then they would be encouraged to clean up the mess with cloths soaked in small buckets of water nearby. What amazed me was not only that children learned quickly how to pour milk or water without spilling and to serve themselves very close to what they wanted or needed to eat, but also that their teachers soon relaxed into those moments of children spilling food and drink. At first, it was a little alarming for teachers who were not used to trusting small children to accomplish these tasks. However, quickly the atmosphere became respectful and calm, and spillages and errors became part of the experience. The setting created an environment of respect. Soon, lunch or snack was a time for everyone to sit together, chat about their day, and break bread together in community.

Praise versus Relationship

In many classrooms around the country, I observe teachers giving attention to children by praising them. It can be anything from a pat on the head to saying, "Good job!" for every little thing a child does to giving stickers for good behavior. In one classroom I observed recently, the teacher handed out pretzels to children who successfully completed a spelling task. She admitted to me as an aside, whispering so that the children could not hear her, that the assignment was so boring that the only way she could get them to complete it was by giving them pretzels.

On the reverse side, time-out, or being isolated from the rest of the group in one way or another, is a punishment that children receive in these same classrooms. Sometimes it is simply because they cannot sit still in a boring, morning meeting, where children are counting how many days they have been in school or being asked to pin a cutout cloud or sun on the weather board. I always wonder at the usefulness of counting how many days children are in school. I understand that it is some sort of math activity. Somehow, though, it reminds me of prisoners crossing off each day they have served out their term! Mind you, we all seem to have survived being treated this way—or have we?

I see all these strategies for praise and punishments as missed opportunities for the development of critical thinking, creating authentic relationships, and cultivating trust between adult and child. For example, there is nothing emptier or more trivializing than saying, "Good job!" for washing hands. After all, what does it mean? Does it take into account that I had to stand on a stool to reach for the faucet, open it to turn on the water, use soap to clean my hands of germs that could make me ill, shake off drops of water, and dry my hands off with the towel? So, first of all, which part was the good job? And as a child, I might wonder, why are all the adults so happy that I washed my hands? Or what do I care that they are happy about that? Actually, it was a chore that I hated doing because it interrupted my playing outside a moment ago with building a mud castle. And, anyway, I might wonder, what is all this excitement about being clean? Clearly, adults are weird people! I'll just do it to please them and stay out of trouble.

In relationship, there is a give-and-take of ideas, listening to one another with respect, and taking seriously what people say to one another. It is not empty or trivial. We relate to one another by validating our experience and extending the conversation, hopefully giving the other person additional food for thought about anything from a mathematics problem to how to share a toy between classmates. We share exciting information and learning how to do a task. We just spend time together when feelings are overwhelming. Life is more complex than just doing a good job, doing what one is told, and staying out of trouble. I want children to learn about communication and caring. I don't want a child to be afraid that I will be angry that she broke a vase. I want her to *care* that pieces of glass are on the floor and someone might cut their foot if she doesn't pick them up. I also want her to know that if she does pick up the pieces, she might cut her hands, so perhaps we could do it carefully together. I want children to think deeply and critically and become intrinsically motivated to do this or that project. I will not be a productive facilitator of learning if children only obey orders so that they can please me or just stay out of trouble. This, for me, has nothing to do with education or relationship.

We enhance children's self-esteem and help them feel worthwhile when they contribute to our society, feel like they belong, and are taken seriously for their ideas and feelings. Lilian Katz (1995) suggests that early childhood teachers are teaching children to be narcissistic, or only worried about themselves, rather than developing self-esteem, which is an authentic understanding of their self-identity. If children are only worried about pleasing adults and staying out of trouble, they are not learning about the complex nature of relationship. In addition, they cannot realistically self-evaluate, because the motivation is completely externalized—outside themselves. Katz gives a simple suggestion for helping children develop their "own criteria of competence": have a child choose which piece of work she would like to share with her parents based on thinking about or discussing whether it "includes all they want it to, or whether they think it is clear or accurate enough, or whether it shows progress compared with the last item they took home." Instead of giving empty praise about everything, "teachers are more likely to foster healthy self-esteem [realistic self-evaluation] when they help children cope with [some] frustration." And I would add, when they talk through things using open-ended questions and allow space for children to reflect on what we are talking about.

In my work with pre-service and in-service teachers, I give them a drawing exercise, after which we talk about what they have created (Jacobson 2008). They are asked to draw anything they like using oil pastels, which create a texturally enhanced feel to their artwork. After hanging their pictures on the wall, each one talks about what she observed in the picture she created. Using gentle, probing questions, I encourage the teachers to talk about their feelings as they describe the stories of their pictures. At times, one of them becomes emotional, recognizing future hopes, shattered dreams, or places and people she missed. Sometimes they cry. As they share their impressions, some begin to identify the importance of the exercise, learning skills, such as listening without judgment to one another as they share personal stories. In addition, they recognize that children's creativity and emotions related to their work are as important as their own.

When we discuss their artwork, I use a series of questions they can replicate with young children. Naturally, my questions for adults are sometimes more sophisticated and my probing further is more complex than what I might use with a young child, but the basic line of questioning remains the same. For example, one of the questions is, "Look at your picture and tell me what you see" (Jacobson 2008, 111). In contrast, when children show their work, teachers often say something like, "How lovely!" or "Good job!" This empty praise closes down conversation and thought processes. In that way, we have decreed—evaluated for the child—how he is to think about his own piece of work. It is good and lovely. End of story. However, when I ask a child (or an adult) to look at his picture and then tell me what *he* sees, he begins to discover colors, shapes, designs, characters, a plot, memories, and dreams for the future, and often he will go on to describe how he would change the drawing or how it makes him feel. After all, it is *his* drawing. Why would I consider interpreting it for him? How can I possibly know what was going through his mind as he planned it, while he created it, or while he looks at it with me? With that simple phrase, "Tell me what you see," I open the door to children's ideas and feelings, extend their learning, and create an opportunity for self-evaluation and reflection. In addition, they learn that I care—really care—and that I want to hear what they think and feel, and how they view their work.

Getting Past Common Thoughts about Toddlers

Toddlers are often described as *terrible twos*. It is that age between older infancy and becoming a three-year-old when adults are most challenged by their behaviors. This is a very important time in human development. It is the time when young toddlers begin to realize that they are separate entities from their caregivers and that they can, in fact, walk or run away down the hall and out of sight.

They discover the taste of independence. And they love it! Confusion and inner conflict arrive, however, when they still need and long for the adults in their lives. Their little legs can carry them away swiftly, and they even find a few words that empower them—like, *No!* However, emotionally, they still depend on the significant adults in their lives. They become torn between wanting independence and needing their adult caregivers so much. It is a bewildering time for adults as well. Distraught and confused parents have said to me things like, "What has happened to my baby? All of a sudden there is this little monster in my home refusing to get dressed, running away, and throwing tantrums for every little decision I make."

In my presentations across the country, over and over again the subject of toddlers arises. People express confusion and frustration and seem to be at their wits' end with these little eighteen-month to three-year-old children whose emotions are raw and explosive. Indeed, this is the beginning of children's search for autonomy and identity. They learn to walk, and toddling away is exciting, exhilarating, and scary—all at the same time. Longing for independence and freedom, toddlers still depend on adults for survival and affection. This inner conflict makes them react in ways that befuddle and enrage the adults who care for them. Toddlers say no to everything we suggest, stamp their feet, and have tantrums for just about everything under the sun. They run away from us and sob desperately if we turn away from them.

All through this phase, I have yet to hear an adult say just how brave and amazing toddlers are. As crazy making as this period of development is, adults still have all the power (we are so much bigger than toddlers physically, for starters!) and ultimately the control over how things will turn out. And yet a typical toddler, about thirty-four inches in height, weighing an average of twenty-eight pounds or so, can stand up, stomp her feet, and say, "No!" very determinedly to a much-larger-than-her adult. This little child literally takes her life in her hands when she does this, for there are some adults who *will* hurt her physically or emotionally in ways I do not care to describe here. This, my friends, is courage—bravery in the face of likely harsh consequences.

Toddlers have to do this. They must test out their will and courage. They are learning to separate, become autonomous, and eventually, to think independently for themselves. At this time, we adults who care for and educate them must stand firm in our unconditional love for them and lean on everything we know about child development to assist them through this critical stage of development. Our attention and connection to them is crucial in understanding what they may be going through. Now is the time for relationship—not punishments and rewards. The truth is that how we accept a toddler's need for autonomy, while at the same time setting boundaries for their safety, will affect them for the rest of their lives. As one of the early childhood education students wrote to me after class one evening, "One thing I learned tonight was the terrible twos represent such a wonderful development of bravery and the beginning of autonomy—they are only being brave not bad."

One Last Thought . . . about Holding Still

When a child is crying or expressing anger or hurt, often our initial response is to do what we experienced in our childhood. Usually this takes the form of some type of control, exclusion, or forced repression of emotions. For example, we exclude children by saying things like, "It is not nice to be angry—go and sit in time-out alone over there until you calm down and are able to be a part of our community." Holding still without judgment of challenging emotions was not often modeled for us when we were children. For young children, being excluded from the classroom community of their peers is lonely, frightening, and hurtful, especially as they are usually confused about what they have done or what was wrong with what they felt at the time. A child forced to swallow down fears or anger in a repressive, exclusionary, and solitary manner only gets rid of the problem temporarily for the teacher. It is bound to return in less productive or conscious ways at different times later in the child's life. My responsibility as an early childhood teacher is to assist and guide children toward self-regulation in inclusive, respectful ways with compassion and wisdom. One of the skills needed for this type of behavior is the ability to hold still and listen without judgment.

Over thirty years ago, when I was a preschool/kindergarten teacher in Israel, I had an assistant who was hardworking and devoted to the children in our classroom. However, whenever a number of children were out sick with the flu, chicken pox, or something else, she would say to me, "Today is the best day ever! There are so few children here today!" I would admonish her gently because I knew she was half-joking. I would say to her, "We wouldn't have a job if they were all out sick!" She would chuckle in response. My assistant teacher was not unusual in her attitude, whether it was in a joke or not. Over the years, I have heard different teachers sigh with relief and say things like that, especially with regard to one or two children in particular. You know—those ones who challenge us with their behaviors. Partly we are relieved because those challenging behaviors make us feel so helpless. Some teachers share with me the feeling that whatever they do may help with the child's behavior for a day or two, but in the end there is nothing left to do.

Teachers also express relief when children stay home because we are taught that children are a nuisance. We have been taught that since we were born and we were children. Children are noisy and in the way when adults have other, more important things to do, and, indeed, once people give birth to children, their entire lifestyle changes. Many adults are excited by that and grateful. But many are not. It is back to that old adage that children should be seen and not heard. They get in the way of the busy adult world. Children speak a different emotional language to adults. We feel guilty if we are unable to discipline them. We have moved passed the imaginary, childlike, fantastical world that children inhabit. Most adults find that sort of behavior or play frivolous. Children tire us out with their neediness. Even teachers feel that way.

I have often thought that although there are many adults who love children and are amazed at how innocent and adorable they are, there are just as many adults who fear children. They are spontaneous, do things impulsively, ask questions we often cannot answer, and express emotions brashly and openly, like, "I hate you! I love you!" Children are messy, noisy, and chaotic, and sometimes we feel like we can't control them without becoming some kind of demon. Adults who were hurt as children fear themselves in their interactions. I had a student once who told me she was afraid to be with children because she was beaten as a child, and she felt like she might not be able to control her urge to hit children in her care. At the end of the course, she wrote to me that she had learned, "You don't have to hurt me to teach me" (Jacobson 2008, 121).

I wonder what it must feel like to be that child whose behaviors constantly upset and irritate the adults around her. I spent most of my childhood being extra careful *not* to upset anyone. I learned early on that expressing my feelings was dangerous because it caused so much anxiety, anger, and stress from my mother. Children can sense when they are not wanted. They are watching us all the time—observing whether we are pleased or angry, and whether it is safe for them to be around us. They need us for their survival especially when they are very young, not only for sustenance and a home but for our approval and love. Therefore, the way we behave and interact with them gives them all sorts of signals about how they might feel. When I was a beginning teacher, fresh out of the teachers' college in Israel, I was aware that children were watching me. I identified with them because I had been good at that when I was a child. I was always on the alert with my mother, looking for signs that the emotional environment was safe for me. I constantly adapted myself according to her feelings. So, as a teacher of young children, I became good at holding still with those who challenged me. I developed faith that with much trial and error, I would eventually figure out a way to resolve emotional issues with children. I would not give up on them.

I remember one five-year-old boy in my class, over forty years ago, who would dissolve into tears whenever anything went wrong. I observed him closely and realized that he would become like an infant. And so I experimented with holding him in my arms, even though he was quite tall for his age and his arms and legs would dangle on the floor as I rocked him back and forth, assuring him everything would be all right. He quickly grew out of that behavior of seemingly falling apart whenever something did not go his way. As I got to know his family better, I understood that he was the youngest of five children and had been brought up mostly by his siblings. He longed for mothering. I did not judge him (or his family) for that. I just tried to give him some of what he was crying for. It worked! The teacher in his preschool class before he arrived in my kindergarten room had warned me that he was a "problem child." I ignored her warnings, as I usually do about children who are coming to me from a different place.

When I was director of the campus children's center, we would receive a number of toddlers who had already been expelled from other programs for biting or other such behaviors that are typical for eighteen-month- to three-year-olds. Mostly, I would not tell our teaching staff how they had come to us. And without exception, we did not have problems with those "refugees" from other early childhood programs. With appropriate curriculum, an understanding of child development, and a determination to try out all sorts of different ways to resolve issues, the teaching staff at our center learned to accept all kinds of behaviors. They had to—I was their director! But they were also willing to try out new approaches, including carrying children on their backs or anything that would resolve a behavior challenge.

Holding still is a strategy. The older I become, the more I am able to hold still with myself. When I was young, I was very hard on myself. I had little patience for my mistakes and flaws. I felt like I was always a nuisance—a burden on everyone. Two books that I read when I was in my late twenties—forty years ago—influenced me deeply, and I still swear by them today. They are about two different child psychologists who held still with children with enormous behavioral and life challenges until they were able to find a way into their secret inner worlds and help them realize themselves. The books are *Dibs in Search of Self* (Axline 1990) and *Children with Emerald Eyes* (Rothenberg 2002). *Dibs in Search of Self* describes how everyone, including parents, teachers, school psychologists, and pediatricians, is "puzzled" by the little boy until Virginia Axline, a play therapist, finds a way through to him. In the foreword to the new edition of *Children with Emerald Eyes*, Peter Levine describes Mira Rothenberg's therapy with deeply disturbed children thus: "[Mira's therapy] is not bound by dogma. Her engagement and rare ability to enter into [the children's] secret inner worlds is a gift that, regrettably, seems less and less available in these times of mechanized quick fixes" (Rothenberg 2002).

I realize that as teachers we are not trained therapists. That is not our job. However, what I found powerful in both those books and what has sustained my work with children and teachers, is the ability to hold still and have faith in the human spirit. That is precisely why I went into this field. It is the resilience and belief that if we try, we can reach any child with any behavior that challenges us emotionally. Children deserve that from us. Nothing is as terrifying, paralyzing, and debilitating as feeling unwanted, a nuisance, or a burden. I suppose that holding still with all kinds of children all my life and having faith that there must be a way to get through to everyone were also my way of healing myself through them. If I did everything I could to reach them, I would redeem my own unwantedness.

Chapter 6

Contemplating Compassion

Everyone responds positively to kindness. . . . Until we are able to look after ourselves, we receive great kindness from many different people, without which we would not survive. Reflecting on this and how we are all just human beings, whether we are rich or poor, educated or uneducated, and whether we belong to one nation, religion, culture or another, may inspire us to repay the kindness we have received by being kind to others ourselves. —The Dalai Lama (preface to Tsabary 2010)

WHAT WITH ONE THING AND ANOTHER, I had been thinking about storms. Perhaps it was the frenzy in my local supermarket as everyone stocked up with food, milk, water—anything—in preparation for the impending power outages, as snow was forecast to start falling early that evening. It was predicted to last for hours, and who knew what might happen? Maybe it was watching at the window as sheets of snow fell endlessly under dark gray skies. It brought out the best in us—cooking up a large pot of nutritious and delicious soup, neighbors teaming up to dig each other out of piles of snow in driveways and on sidewalks. Forced to stay indoors, I met new challenges, including how to just do nothing and sitting on the couch in front of the television screen like a robotic zombie, staring at weather reports.

The night before, I had dreamed of high seas and rolling waves—especially the kind of tsunami-like wave that rises up high suddenly and crashes over walls, swallowing up crowds. I woke up and lay quietly in bed wondering about storms: the calm or frenzy before, and picking up the pieces to return to old routines after. Are we always just the same after a storm? Or have we learned something? Did the trauma and exhilaration change us? Or do we pick ourselves up and move on as if nothing has happened? I am always amazed at how I survive over and over again. I have lived through snow, rain, and thunderstorms, divorce and death storms, health scare storms, breaking up with darling friends, losing people I thought I would never lose. Storms within and without.

Each time, picking up the pieces has a different feel. Sometimes I limp for a while or stretch out bruised hands from bashing at piles of ice blocking access to our driveway. There have been times when my heart felt broken and I feared I would never smile again. After the storm, I see torn and broken azalea plants and trees with shattered limbs, and yet when the sun shines feebly through the weakening clouds, I seem to rise up over and over again, returning to old, familiar routines—feeding the cats, watering plants, answering telephones and texts—and I face the new day with some small, renewed sense of patience, understanding, or even wisdom. Although all that becomes clear much later.

Caring for Children Is Hard Emotional Work

While I was writing this book, our neighbors invited me to dinner when my husband was out of town. As is usual whenever I am writing a book, the conversation came around to what the subject of my latest project was. "So, what is your book about?" came the question, and I responded, "Everyone needs attention." Our neighbor, who knows me well, said, "That's an easy one for you, Tamar. Chapter

1: Everyone needs attention; chapter 2: I mean it—*everyone* needs attention; chapter 3: I *really* mean it; and the final chapter: I mean it even more—everyone needs attention!" We laughed, I especially, because I realized that much of each chapter of this book reflects my urgent call to teachers and parents—to all adults who care for and educate young children—to heed this: *I really mean it,* everyone needs attention. Or to put it a different way, as I said to the conference workshop attendees some months ago: everyone needs *relationship,* including teachers and caregivers.

I reach for a beloved book that I acquired a couple of decades ago and reread a new edition in a revised format: *Teaching Four-Year-Olds,* by Carol Hillman (2010). In her appreciation for teachers and caregivers, she writes:

> I have the highest regard for both teachers and caregivers. Upon their shoulders lies the daunting task of nurturing the next generation. It is they who grapple with the requirements and expectations for the schooling of these youngsters. It is they who live their lives as role models, and put forth infinite energy and wisdom in doing so. Teachers and caregivers are the bedrock of our society. They are the unsung cultural leaders of our time. (20–21)

I could not agree with Hillman more. Working with children is a tough job, especially from the point of view that you have to be "on" constantly, relating to every child in your classroom. Enid Elliot (2007) describes this as a "variety of pulls on [caregivers'] time, emotion and energy. . . . Establishing and maintaining a caring and responsive relationship calls for a variety of skills and calls forth myriad emotions"(2). Children constantly need and want a lot—nay, all—of our attention. Of course, no one can be *on* 100 percent of the time, twenty-four hours a day. Children do need to learn that. Adults need to know that, too, and have compassion for themselves when working or being with children. In addition, not every slight or difficult interaction will ruin someone for life. D. W. Winnicott (1986), a renowned English pediatrician and psychoanalyst, says that we can be "good enough." While he is describing an infant's relationship with her mother, we can apply his theory to our own work with children:

> The good-enough "mother" (not necessarily the infant's own mother) is one who makes active adaptation to the infant's needs, and active adaptation that gradually lessens, according to the infant's growing ability to account for failure of adaptation and to tolerate the results of frustration. (10)

In other words, it is important for a child to be able to tolerate some frustration and not receive immediate gratification, but we should be empathetic and respectful in how we teach that. Winnicott goes on to explain that the mother lessens her full sacrifice (going without sleep, giving up her every need) "gradually, according to the infant's growing ability to deal with her failure"(10). In fact, an important part of a child's development is coming to understand that frustration has a time limit. In addition, while the child learns to tolerate frustration, she develops imagination by remembering the past and fantasizing about what will happen next when the caregiver returns.

A little frustration helps young children become autonomous and learn how to solve problems on their own as they gradually enter the adult world and become part of the society and culture they live in. The main point here is the word *gradually,* and I would add, according to children's emotional development. Within all our theories and prescriptions about what we should and should not do, we must remember that we are dealing with human beings—each one with a unique set of experiences, genetics, and cultures. So, even the term *gradually* can be confusing, because it has different meanings for people in various contexts. Human relationships are as complex as can be. What feels gradual for some could be really slow going for others, or not gradual enough.

Guilt Is a Harsh Taskmaster

Many years ago, a former graduate student reconnected with me. When I knew her as a student, she was in her midtwenties and newly married. She was a quiet person, observant and wise for her age, and an excellent teacher of young children because she related well to them by listening carefully and validating their feelings. I was excited to meet her again, especially because I had heard that she had two children of her own. I imagined I would find her enthusiastic and happy to be a parent herself. After the usual hugs and smiles and excitement at reconnecting with one another, we sat down to drink coffee and eat pastries. We had so much to tell each other to catch up with the years that had passed.

Before long, she was describing her life to me. She told me of the challenges and difficulties she faced with two young children. She poured out her heart to me, saying that she wished someone had warned her of how hard mothering would be. She had set high standards for herself as a parent, especially since she had studied child development in her graduate school courses. She found that she was constantly feeling guilty about her feelings of anger and dismay at her young children's behaviors. At one point, she turned to me and said, "Someone should write a book called *A Handbook of Guilt for Parents*!" We both laughed out loud, she through the tears in her eyes. I became quiet and put my hand on hers. "Perhaps I'll write it for you one day," I said. For a long time now, I have wanted to write that book. It would be humorous, filled with anecdotes from my life as a parent, including other people's stories if they wanted to share them as well. The idea would be to alleviate the guilt we all have because of how hard it is to work with young children and how much we all crave to get it right! Here is an anecdote right now in honor of always having to get it right with the young children in our care.

One Saturday morning, my husband and I went to our local coffee shop early. We had gotten out of bed at four thirty in preparation for a flight to Seattle. Our bags were packed and out on the front porch awaiting the taxi, when at five o'clock my phone rang with a call from the airlines to inform me that the flight had been canceled. While bleary-eyed and still a little sleepy, I quietly chatted with the woman on the phone and rescheduled our flight for the afternoon. After some reorganizing, we decided it was time for an early-morning trip for coffee. A cappuccino was sounding pretty good to me right about the moment that my husband made the suggestion.

Our usually popular coffee shop was quiet. A few early-morning people like us were sprinkled around the room, some reading newspapers, others gazing at computer screens. We picked up our drinks and some piping hot egg-white sandwiches from the barista—comfort food to help us plan the unexpectedly free morning we had received through the cancellation of our flight. We sank into two comfortable armchairs and devoured the breakfast sandwiches as if we had not seen food for a long, long time. It felt good.

After some munching and slurping, I noticed a man and woman sitting around a table close by. They were intent on feeding some breakfast items to a young toddler. The little fellow toddled around the table and then ran behind and in between their chairs. Whenever he reappeared by their table, they would hastily shove morsels of food into his mouth. He giggled and waddled away. By then I assumed that the adults were his parents. The child wore pajamas, and his feet were covered in soft, colorful sock-type slippers decorated with pale-blue floral patterns. Every now and then he would stand on his tiptoes and then run around again and again. His fluid movements and his parents' pleasure in his joy mesmerized me. They seemed like such a contented trio.

Finally, while they were gathering up their things preparing to leave, the toddling boy stopped by close to me and stared into my eyes. "Hi!" I greeted him, and he smiled. "I love your slippers," I said. He seemed to like hearing that. He shook his head from side to side, giggled, and stomped his feet as if in a dance. His mother smiled at me as well, and then she said almost by way of apology, "Yes, they are the easiest things to get on his feet because he moves so quickly. I know they probably are not the best for his feet. No support and all that. But they are the easiest." She laughed nervously. I tried to put her at ease, repeating that I thought they were a great choice. They all hurried out, keeping up with the mercurial rhythm of their young child. This mother had seemed so joyful about her little toddler's escapades, and then this strange older woman (me) came along and, oh dear, mentioned the slippers—those dreaded slippers. As I watched them leaving the coffee shop, I couldn't help but think how parents constantly feel guilty. The young woman had seemed ever so slightly embarrassed—or was it ashamed?—of her choice of shoes for her child, and I almost felt sorry I had mentioned them at all. I wondered who had been the first to nurture her guilt about those slippers as bad for her son's feet. Was it her mother, siblings, father, extended family members, or in-laws? Perhaps other women friends, or maybe she had read something in a parenting book.

I understood her, of course. I had been a mother of a toddler once. And I remember all too well those guilty, shameful moments when I felt like the choices I made were the "wrong" ones. It was usually when I was with my mother or mother-in-law, and at times with friends, who always seemed to know how to parent so much better than I. If only I could have run after that loving family, with the colorfully slippered, quick-footed toddler. I would have said to them, "Don't be guilty or ashamed. Cherish the joy you were expressing right before I opened my mouth to speak. You are really great parents, full of care and love for this bright little fellow! And as for your choice of slippers? Well . . . just perfect!"

We Are Tested with Our Responses When There Are Strong Emotions

As a mother and a teacher, how many times have I felt helpless and incompetent when trying to communicate with a child who is overwhelmed with emotion for one reason or another? We are tested over and over again with our responses when children display strong emotions. And in the end, most of us seem to survive our childhoods in remarkable ways. Human beings are as resilient as can be. Perhaps, one day I will write a book for parents and teachers that alleviates everyone from the guilt of being a good-enough parent and of getting it right. As much as we have knowledge about child development and are aware of how our own childhood experiences may influence our interactions and behaviors, still, once we are in the field with many unique, emotional little individuals, we are often overwhelmed by not knowing what to do. Have compassion for yourself! A mistake or two here and there will not harm anyone for life. You can always go home and write about it or reflect on what happened. I have gone back the next day and apologized. That did not make me look weak or out of control. In fact, it mostly strengthened my relationships with children and coworkers. Most people just crave validation, and everyone needs hope and faith that we can resolve issues together. An authentic, heartfelt apology can go a long way.

Developing Compassionate Relationships

Over the years, I have observed many teachers interacting with young children with empathy and compassion: talking to them, holding them, wiping away tears, listening and responding as they expanded children's learning and gave them skills to understand, express, and accept their emotions. Each time I observed their careful and intentional interactions, I was in awe of these teachers and grateful for what they did for the children in their classrooms. How did they know how to do this, I wonder? Was it from classes, reading, observing others, their own childhood memories, or was it innate, just a part of their makeup? Can adults be taught empathy and compassion even if they did not experience it themselves? Is putting myself in someone else's shoes a skill I can learn, just like tying my shoes? Or does a person have to suffer in order to understand another's suffering? And even if we don't really understand another's suffering, can we imagine what it *might* be like to be that person? With small children, the trick is realizing that even though they are less sophisticated than adults intellectually or physically, their feelings are as real and meaningful as any we have—different perspectives in different proportions perhaps, but they are feelings nevertheless.

In my workshops, during my presentations, and in my books, I tell my story about how I understand my childhood, and how I learned to make connections between my personal life and the professional decisions I make in the field of early childhood education. I do this so that you, the reader, who is interested in caring for and educating young children might do the same for yourself. I think that honing this specific self-reflection skill will help you to become more empathic and compassionate. The only problem is that you have to be prepared to dive in deep and really learn about your life and how you *felt* as a child about anything and everything. You have to be prepared to confront discomfort and pain as well as remember joys and excitement. While I recognize my mother's flaws and her own difficult life, and forgive her the pain she inadvertently or intentionally caused me, I must still validate that these things happened to me in order to understand that I was not to blame for them. This helps me in my work with children because I am able to put myself in their shoes. I know how it feels to yearn for mothering, to long to be noticed, to be afraid, confused, alone, rejected, and betrayed. As Alice Miller writes:

> Only by knowing the truth can we be set free. Only in this way can we free ourselves from the fears and anxieties we knew as children, blamed and punished for sins we did not know we had committed, the fateful fear of the sin of disobedience, that crippling anxiety that has wrecked so many people's lives and keeps them in thrall to their own childhood. (Miller 2001, 9)

Last year I was visiting one of our student teachers in her school placement. I arrived at the preschool room just as naptime was ending and children were waking up. Most of the children had gotten up, had put away their blankets and cots, and were heading out to the playground. One little girl was still lying on her cot, staring out at all of us. She looked relaxed and comfortable and in no rush to leave her sleeping space. I watched as the cooperating teacher walked slowly over to her and said, "Well, are you ready to get up?" The child shook her head in refusal. The teacher gave her a warm smile and responded quietly, "When you're ready. Take your time." I thought of all the times I had heard other teachers in this similar position, with a strict time schedule to be obeyed, scolding, threatening, or shaming, saying things like, "If you don't get up, you won't be able to go outside. You'll miss snack. It's time to get up. Get up!" and on and on. Quite soon after this brief interaction with her teacher, the girl looked at me and smiled. She showed me the soft toy she had with her on the cot. We discussed the toy for a few brief moments—its name, how long she'd had it, what she loved about it—and then she rose up, stretched and yawned, put her things away, and skipped out onto the playground.

With kindness and respect, the child was given space to wake up at her own pace. Nothing was too urgent or important to come before that. As a result, she reacted with friendship and grace. During that same semester, another student told me how the children in her classroom had to get up immediately after naptime. One little boy was having a difficult time waking up, and she tried to comfort him. The cooperating teacher swooped in and whisked his cot and blanket away. He was left sitting on the floor staring into space as if he were shell-shocked. The student cried about how the boy was treated when she related the story to me. Different kinds of attention for different kinds of children. What had happened in that cooperating teacher's life that made her treat that preschooler in that manner, I wondered. Would she treat another adult or a friend like that? What was so urgent in the schedule that the child would have missed? Snacktime? Outdoor play? A story? What?

Erika Christakis (2016) writes about how testing and standards have taken away play and hands-on learning environments for young children, and how structured and abstract teaching has become. She is concerned that we have taken away children's natural learning "habitat" and that taking away children's ability to connect and explore is a "real threat to our society's future." Christakis invites us to be empathetic. She says, "Most of our problems can be addressed simply by seeing those things in young children that have remained stubbornly unseen. We can solve our child-rearing and teaching challenges quite easily by looking more closely at what preschoolers can and can't do. Our first step is to walk into a classroom and see it from their view."(31) Christakis starts off the second chapter of her book with "Step into a four-year-old's shoes and what will you find when you walk into a typical preschool classroom?" (33). This is an eye-opening chapter indeed, because she shows us exactly what it must *feel* like for children in that setting.

We can learn about empathy through reading examples like these. Looking through the eyes of children and "seeing children" in every different context of their lives teach us how it *feels* to be a young child (Curtis 2017). And yet somehow, even after reading such enlightening examples of empathetic awareness, so many of us go back to doing what was done to us over and over again. What is it about self-reflection and change that is such a struggle? I know people who loathe the very thought of looking back to their own childhood for guidance. They say, "Let go of the past! Be here now!" They see it as a way of blaming our parents for the choices we make as adults. "Why dig it up and rehash all that stuff?" they ask. And yet we always say that we learn from history—we can learn from our mistakes. Could we look back on our childhood without blaming anyone? Rather, in learning from our own childhood history, we seek validation for what we experienced. I have found that when I validate my experience and allow myself to really feel the feelings, I am then able to let go and forgive. If it is all bottled up and stifled within, I become stuck, paralyzed, and unable to change my mind:

> Facing uncomfortable feelings of loneliness, anger, or jealousy cleared the way for me to see my parents as people with difficulties, frailties, and vulnerabilities of their own. In that way, I could [free myself up] to realize the strengths and characteristics I love and admire about them. . . . This type of reflection helps us [as well] when we interact with children. . . . We develop compassion and empathy the more we understand and accept uncomfortable feelings about ourselves. (Jacobson 2003, 125)

Self-Reflection and Changing Our Worldview

Our mind was set a long time ago—back in our childhoods—and changing our minds is a difficult process indeed (Dweck 2016). According to Carol Dweck (2016), children need to feel worthy and loved, and when they become unsure or anxious about whether they are valued, they create a "fixed mindset" where they imagine themselves as being someone different whom their parents could like better. To change, we need to develop a "growth mindset" that will ask us to give up our fixed mind-sets:

> As you can imagine, it's not easy to just let go of something that has felt like your "self" for many years and that has given you your route to self-esteem. And it's especially not easy to replace it with a mindset that tells you to embrace all the things that have felt threatening: challenge, struggle, criticism, setbacks. (Dweck 2016, 235)

Dweck reminds us that change is not like surgery, because we can't replace our old beliefs with a new part, like we do with hip and knee replacements. She suggests that "new beliefs take their place alongside the old ones, and as they become stronger, they give you a different way to think, feel, and act" (224). We can all change our mind-sets from fixed to growth, as long as we understand that change takes time. It is an incremental process with many regressive moments, especially when things get tough emotionally.

I like to call my fixed mind-set an emotional life script (Jacobson 2008). It was a way of seeing reality mostly through my mother's view of me but also through my own repeated patterns of behavior, which reinforced my script. Rewriting my emotional script and changing my mind-set are not always easy. Sometime ago my therapist suggested that learning a new reality of myself is like taking off sunglasses to see the world in different shades and colors. It can feel confusing, cause us insecurities, and is often painful. Some of us welcome change with all its challenges and struggles. Others feel anxious and resistant—even fearful or filled with resentment. Do I have to do this? All these different feelings are natural if we decide to change our mind-set and rewrite the emotional life script.

Learning-about-ourselves reflection is essential for becoming more intentional in our teaching (Heidemann, Menniga, and Chang 2016). Lindy Austin (2009) describes self-reflection as empowering, saying that "reflection of personal experience is empowering for learners because they confront the contradictions of everyday life" (160). Deb Curtis (2017) describes using a "thinking lens for reflective teaching" that includes five ways "to deepen the practice of observing children" (11). I mention the first one specifically because it is related to reflective practice. It is called knowing yourself.

Knowing yourself

- How am I reacting to this situation and why?
- What in my background and values is influencing my response to this situation and why?
- What adult perspectives (standards, health and safety, time, goals) are on my mind?

Honoring our profession, we develop ways to become more professional. Self-reflection helps us understand why we do what we do and helps us become more intentional. If we develop a growth mind-set, we give ourselves a variety of options to choose from. If we were not given opportunities to develop empathy and compassion or if we have not witnessed these qualities throughout our early childhood, we may find it difficult to hone those skills once we are set in our worldview of children and education. But we can always change if we set our mind to it! And if we have chosen to care for and educate young children, we have a responsibility to become intentional, to avoid hurting them as much as we can.

The Answers Lie within You

As we reach the end of this book, you may be frustrated to discover that I don't have specific answers, prescriptions, or magic solutions to the challenges you face as teachers or as parents with children who constantly demand your attention. I also don't have magic recipes for helping the withdrawn or quiet children who need your attention as much, if not more, than those who brazenly demand it. There are a couple of reasons I have chosen not to give you a prescription or list of things to do.

The first reason is that there are many books and programs that give you specific strategies with a number of prescribed steps you can take to teach children self-regulation. Early childhood and behavior and classroom management experts who have created these programs or written about this are certain that if you take a number of prescribed steps, you will acquire the desired outcome: children who are able to self-regulate, teachers who can manage their classrooms, and parents who will have well-behaved children. Many of these programs, books, and articles are helpful. They give constructive guidelines that help us understand how children need boundaries and limits as they learn to deal with delayed gratification and become members of our adult society. Using positive types of guidance techniques, we learn to help children resolve issues on their own and deal with the frustrations that everyday life offers us.

The second reason I do not give you a prescribed list of steps is that I believe the answer lies within you. As I have discussed, I believe it's very important to get to know how you feel about children needing your attention. I suggest that by holding still with yourself, journaling and self-reflecting, you can find out about what is happening within you and with your own emotions that is affecting your interaction with a specific child. You may find that a child reminds you of someone you did not like in your past or a sibling you had conflicts with, or even that she reminds you of yourself.

In my courses, students are required to do a child observation project where they observe the developmental progress of a child of their choosing during the four-month semester at their internship site. One of the main points when writing up their report for me is to explain why they chose the child, what drew them to that specific person, what they liked or did not like, what intrigued them, and what they wanted to know more about that child. Often, students describe the child as reminding them of themselves—as quiet or withdrawn as they were/are, or as spunky and feisty as they were/are.

The steps you are trying to take have been prescribed by someone for whom the process succeeded. This work is so much more powerful than that. By the way, experts don't always tell us about the many times their strategies did *not* work for them or about the many times they felt helpless or overwhelmed by the intense outbursts of children's emotional expression—because each child is unique, and there is no one size that fits all. In a support-supervision group I facilitated many years ago, one of the teachers was challenged by an angry four-year-old in her classroom whom she disliked and was sure disliked her (Jacobson 2003). Processing her feelings of anger with our group, the teacher revealed to us that the child reminded her of a man from a difficult relationship in her past. In the final group session, she said,

> Remember that struggle I had about that thing with the angry stuff I had with him? By working through it here, some of it, I was able to then work with him in a different way. . . . And I was saying that when he found out that I wasn't gonna be the teacher in the room anymore, he was jumping up and down going: "No, you can't go! No, you can't go!" I looked at him, and said, "T.H. is that you?" I couldn't believe it. Obviously, we had gotten somewhere because he would never have done that, I don't think. (Jacobson 2003, 101)

When the support group ended, group members expressed feeling more comfortable with emotions in general, and they shared that they felt more accepting of children's emotions. They expressed that this also "directly affected a change in behaviors toward children in their classrooms" (Jacobson 2003).

Of course, I would love nothing more than to be able to facilitate more of these types of support groups for teachers who are willing to learn how to make connections between their own emotions and how that affects their relationships with children. However, I invite you to start developing those skills on your own or with other colleagues who are willing to listen to you without judgment, and perhaps you can talk through how various emotions affect how you view children's needing your attention—how you can improve your relationships with children in your care.

Here are some questions that may help you get in touch with your feelings as you start to do this work:

- How do your childhood experiences influence you? What buttons do they push?
- How have you faced your own discomfort about remembering what angered and hurt you as a child about being ignored or rejected, or receiving attention?
- Were you overwhelmed with joy when someone noticed your effort and shared that with you when you were a child?
- Were you filled with dismay and resentment when you were overlooked or rejected?
- How did it feel to be excluded or when something seemed unfair?
- How have you validated your own experience?

Bruce Perry reminds us that we cannot love ourselves, feel valued, and develop healthy self-esteem and self-worth alone, without support:

> For years, mental health professionals taught people that they could be psychologically healthy without social support, that "unless you love yourself, no one else will love you." . . . People without any relationships were believed to be as healthy as those who had many. These ideas contradict the fundamental biology of human species: we are social mammals, and could never have survived without deeply interconnected and

> interdependent human contact. The truth is, you cannot love yourself unless you have been loved and are loved. The capacity to love cannot be built in isolation. (Perry and Szalavitz 2006, 234)

Conclusion

One of the things I have learned about myself while writing this book is that I love receiving attention. I have come a long way psychologically to feeling comfortable declaring that outright without guilt or shame. One of the ways I realized this recently was right outside my house on the sidewalk. My husband and I are fortunate to live in a fine home with a large yard, where I have cultivated a garden full of many species of plants, shrubs, and trees. Indeed, as I was writing about this in our library on the second floor, I looked out the window at two tall crepe myrtle trees that over the past seven years have reached high up, creating a loving arch between them laced with big, velour, pink blossoms. A hummingbird darted between the flowers and distracted me from writing this story down. Our home, although set a ways back from the road, is situated on a main thoroughfare where during the day traffic whizzes by noisily and at top speed even though the speed limit is twenty-five miles per hour. On the day that I wrote this, I took a break from writing and went down to our sidewalk to remove weeds that had started growing off into the road.

As I bent down to pull on the weeds, a car sped down the road across from us and turned onto the main street, pulling suddenly to a halt next to me while traffic behind it started to pile up. I stood up and stared at the woman in the car, who rolled down the passenger side window to talk to me. "Is this your house?" she called out to me. "Yes," I said. I noticed the grimaces and angry faces in the cars behind her. "I just had to stop and tell you how much I love your garden. I just had to tell you how much pleasure I get from it each day I drive by here." I beamed at her. "Thank you so much," I responded, feeling warmth and joy well up in my heart.

Someone had noticed my garden, me, and my efforts and had taken the trouble to tell me, even backing up traffic to do so. I stood still a moment, overjoyed and a little overwhelmed. Then I laughed out loud and said to myself, "I do love receiving attention. In fact, everyone needs attention." I walked quickly upstairs to the library to write this down so that I didn't forget. As I was in the middle of sharing this incident with you, the doorbell rang. I walked downstairs and opened the front door to find a large bouquet of flowers. I gasped in surprise and went directly to the kitchen to find an appropriate vase for them. I discovered from the gift card that the flowers were sent to me from my daughter-in-law. She wrote, "Just a little bouquet of flowers in case of cloudy moments on the book-writing journey."

At that point, tears of gratitude and joy were filling my eyes. First the woman telling me my garden brings her pleasure, then the bouquet of flowers in case of cloudy moments. As I was feeling overwhelmed with all this attention, my husband suggested we go out for brunch to celebrate. We drove to our favorite part of town to a beloved restaurant, and as we sauntered along the sidewalk, I found a quarter right next to my foot. I bent down to pick it up. "A straight three!" I exclaimed, laughing, and immediately remembered a friend of mine who would probably say something like, "The Universe is watching out for you." I responded to her in my mind, "The Universe is paying attention to me today." I embraced the universe with open arms. We need all the attention we can get!

In 2003, when I was writing my first book (2003), I wrote a whole chapter about the importance of compassion. Now, fifteen years later, I still hold out for it. Growing up, I cared about my mother deeply, as if she were my child, and when I left her in Israel thirty years ago to emigrate to the United States, I always felt as if I had abandoned or betrayed her. I was not the mother to my son that I might have been if I had known then what I know now. I made my share of mistakes as a mother, wife, and teacher. Relationships are complex—they are never easy.

When stormy emotional rivers have thrashed around me, I have hung on for dear life to compassion and gratitude. They have always steered me through to the other side—to calmer waters of acceptance and love. As teachers, children give us work, passion, and inspiration. They will love us with all their might if we pay attention to them with an open heart. If we watch them closely, we can learn about emotions, spontaneity, joy for life, curiosity, and ourselves, for we relive our own childhoods over and over again, each time redeeming our own selves through their first-time discoveries and expressions of amazement.

Be grateful for them.

Forgive them.

Love them with all your might.

Of all the issues and challenges that early childhood education faces as a field, I have chosen to focus on children's emotional development. I want children to get a better deal emotionally than I had. However, many adults were emotionally wounded as young children. So I have chosen to focus on everyone's emotional development, especially of those who intentionally care for and educate young children. As we uncover the hurt we have endured as young children ourselves, we free ourselves to be accepting, authentic, and present for children in our care. Thus, we are able to be more intentional with our interactions and behaviors in ways that help children achieve a sense that they are valued and loved—crucial for developing self-esteem and self-worth. I have chosen to make a stand on all of this for the sake of children.

As Lilian Katz (2014) says:

> Teaching involves many conflicting pressures and situations. We cannot respond fully or equally to all of them. . . . We have to decide what's worth making an issue over. Select those issues that really matter to you. . . . And then, take your stand with clarity, with confidence, and courage for the sake of the children.

Epilogue

After years of therapy and over the course of writing this book, I have come to understand that my mother's treatment of me was emotionally abusive and that she was as flawed a person as anyone I know. However, I am aware that she was a product of her own childhood traumas. For example, she was sent to boarding school far from home when she was just six years old. Even as all my life I yearned for her attention and mothering, I also learned a lot from my mother's strengths and have always loved that she was a nonconformist, well read, charismatic, and passionate.

Six months after my mother died, I was sifting through old papers in my memory box and found a correspondence between my mother and me from 2001. I think that my letter to her then was a tribute to her, and I wish I had read it aloud at her funeral.

On November 17, 2001, I wrote the following:

Dear Mom,

I have been thinking about you a lot. I thought about how much you always helped others and how you enjoy life through all your suffering. I see in myself pieces of you, and I am so proud and happy that you are my mother. My strength, determination. The fact that I help anyone—doesn't matter who they are, where they come from, how much it costs, or how risky it will be. That comes from you. My ability to not just accept what someone tells me—but check it out (research it!)—that comes from you. Although you were not a major political activist, I learned from you that injustice and intolerance are not right. I learned about brutal honesty from you! And I love that. I learned from you that one could always make things better. Even in my darkest hours, I always find a way out. I learned that from you. Money is no object! I learned that from you. Love of—no not love—passion for music, I learned from you. Passion for drama, I learned from you. All these wonderful pieces of you are inside me. I own them and have made them a part of me. And I am the richer for it. And so is my son.

I know that you and I—our relationship—have been challenged through the years. So many struggles and fights. But my love for you is strong and I am deeply grateful for so much of what I have learned from you. I admire your courage, Mom. You tirelessly search for happiness and find it in beautiful moments, beautiful gardens, beautiful books, movies, with interesting people, and with children. You taught us all to love children—to respect children—and to fight for them. Each of us fights for our children in our family in deep, respectful ways. Sometimes the love and fight for our children seems weird—but we all know that our children are the most precious. You taught us all that.

You are a work of art, Mom. And I cherish and appreciate you so much. I am writing you this letter in a gorgeous hotel in a beautiful wooded, parklike area of Washington, D.C. It is early in the morning—sun shining through the windows and beautiful fall leaves—red, orange, rust colored, are brilliant with the sun's rays. I will meet with the book editor today at noon to see what he has to offer/suggest. And I remember you giving me a typewriter for my 16th birthday! What a gift that was. I wish I had held on to it all those years. You taught me that writing, knowledge, education is so important. You were right! And I have learned that it is very important to be yourself no matter what. It's tough. It makes people mad, and we lose people along the way who can't take it—but being who we are is more important than anything.

Am going to do my workout and prepare for my meeting. I am so excited. And you are the only person I felt like sharing this with! I always remember you sitting by my bed when I was little and you would tell me the story of how, one day, I would dance at Covent Garden, and you would be up in the box watching. Well, today sort of feels like that story.

I love you, Mom. Thank you.

Tamar

A month later, on December 19, 2001, my mother wrote me a letter in response. Here is part of it:

My darling Tamar,

Here I am in Manchester—it was lovely to find your pig on arrival [my mother loved pigs and I had sent her a picture of one] *and he is on my table now instead of one of the family! Did you get my message on your phone the other day before I left? I travelled on British Airways and had to change planes in London as there isn't a direct flight anymore—perfect attention from start to finish and tasty fresh food—so different from Air Canada. This letter is meant to be an answer to the overwhelming letter that you sent me—the one that I am most terrified to touch. When I go back I intend to read it quite often and get used to it and what it offers. There have been many times in my life that I felt I was standing alone on top of a cold mountain with big winds roaring around—I am not being dramatic as I am not a morbid person. That is just the way I felt, but now your letter has made me feel a warm, soft blanket wrapped around me and great security. I wanted to write something down so that when I am dead you will have something to hold and look at and you will remember this happy time we had together. The telephone conversation is not solid enough. It will fade away.*

[She then went on to describe news about her life in Israel and her visit in Manchester. She concluded:]

Happy Xmas and New Year—special love to [my son and husband] *xxx*

As ever

B/Mom [My mother's name was Beryl, but she often referred to herself as B when she was with close friends. In this letter she signed off as B and Mom (B/Mom)—further accentuating the complexity of our relationship, I believe.]

The pain I have been feeling since my mother's death has surprised me because I thought I had worked it all out between us. But, somehow, the end of her life has given me permission to allow myself to experience feelings—feelings that I had stifled during my childhood in order to survive and continue a loving relationship with my mother going forward. I realize without doubt that we loved each other and that we competed with one another, as women often do.

While I will continue to write and feel like I have the last word when it comes to my version of our relationship, I feel happily and with much emotion that my mother has the last word in her moving response to my letter many years ago in 2001, on the eve of my becoming a published author.

She knew that putting words in writing would give me something to hold on to when she died. That is a testament to her understanding of life and to the fierce, complicated love she had for all her children—me included.

Appendix

Questions to Reflect on as You Do the Work

- How did you develop your worldview?
- Who were your role models or mentors?
- What were some of the ways you sought out attention when you were a child?
- How did the significant adults in your life react to your needing attention?
- Think about why you might trivialize someone. In other words, why do you not take them seriously? For example, why when a child or adult tells you something serious and important, do you respond with how cute they are, change the subject, or laugh about what they are saying? Are you jealous of them? Does what they say seem absurd to you? Do you feel inferior to them? Do you not have the time to hear them through? How do we learn to listen to children and take them seriously if we have never experienced that ourselves when we were children?
- What does it feel like to be trivialized? Can you remember a time when that happened to you and how it made you feel? Put yourself in another person's shoes: for example, how do you feel when others do not take you seriously? This is

empathy—putting yourself in someone else's shoes. Where and how did you learn empathy? Who taught it to you?

- What do you know about compassion? How did it feel for you when someone was compassionate with you?
- How did it feel for you when someone listened to you and related to what you were saying or feeling?
- How can we allow children to talk through something with us without interpreting or putting words in their mouths because we think we have the answer—or even if we do have the answer?
- Think about how you understand the idea of "self-regulation." Why do you think it is important for children to self-regulate? How did you learn to self-regulate when you were a child?
- When you were a child, how did you react to punishments?
- How do you react to painful childhood memories?
- How do you validate your own need for attention?
- What do you remember about your own childhood story?
- What events or incidents stand out for you as important in your emotional development?
- Who can you interview about your earliest childhood?
- How do you think your own emotional life script affects your behaviors and interactions with young children in your care?

References

Austin, Lindy. 2009. "Reflective Teaching Strategies for a Reflective Educator." In *Conversations on Early Childhood Teacher Education: Voices from the Working Forum for Teacher Educators*, edited by Andrew Gibbons and Colin Gibbs. Redmond, WA: World Forum Foundation.

Axline, Virginia M. 1977. *Play Therapy*. New York: Ballantine Books.

———. 1990. *Dibs in Search of Self*. New York: Ballantine Books.

Barrett, Lisa Feldman. 2017. *How Emotions Are Made: The Secret Life of the Brain*. New York: Houghton Mifflin Harcourt Publishing Company.

Bierman, Karen, Mark T. Greenberg, and Rachel Abenavoli. 2017. *Promoting Social and Emotional Learning in Preschool: Programs and Practices That Work*. Edna Bennett Pierce Prevention Research Center, Pennsylvania State University.

ChildCareExchange. Ed.flicks: Exchange Training Videos on Demand, www.childcareexchange.com/ed-flicks.

Christakis, Erika. 2016. *The Importance of Being Little: What Preschoolers Really Need from Grownups*. New York: Viking.

Christie, Toni. 2011. *Respect: A Practitioner's Guide to Calm and Nurturing Infant Care and Education*. Wellington, NZ: Childspace Early Childhood Institute.

———. 2017. Keynote address, International Infant Toddler Conference, Tulsa, OK, April 6.

Curtis, Deb. 2017. *Really Seeing Children*. Lincoln, NE: Exchange Press.

Dombro, Amy Laura, Judy Jablon, and Charlotte Stetson. 2011. *Powerful Interactions: How to Connect with Children to Extend Their Learning*. Washington, DC: National Association for the Education of Young Children.

Dweck, Carol S. 2016. *Mindset: The New Psychology of Success*. New York: Ballantine Books.

Elliot, Enid. 2007. *We're Not Robots: The Voices of Daycare Providers*. SUNY Series, Early Childhood Education: Inquiries and Insights. Albany: State University of New York Press.

Ferholt, Beth, Sonja De Groot Kim, Alexandra Miletta, Liege Motta, Amy Snider, Wendy Pollock, and Rick Ellis. 2015. "Professors Reflect Conference, Piecing Together a Future for American Education: A Conversation about Reggio Emilia with Local Professors." Stephen Wise Free Synagogue Early Childhood Center, New York City, February 5.

Gartrell, Dan. 2016. Quoted in ExchangeEveryDay, "The Challenge of Aggression," March 23. www.childcareexchange.com/eed/issue/4090.

Gerhardt, Sue. 2004. *Why Love Matters: How Affection Shapes a Baby's Brain*. Hove, East Sussex, NY: Brunner-Routledge.

Harper, Laurie J. 2016. "Preschool through Primary Grades: Using Picture Books to Promote Social-Emotional Literacy." *Young Children* 71, no. 3 (July): 80–86.

Heidemann, Sandra, Beth Menninga, and Claire Chang. 2016. *The Thinking Teacher: A Framework for Intentional Teaching in the Early Childhood Classroom.* Golden Valley, MN: Free Spirit Publishing.

Hillman, Carol B. 2010. *Teaching Four-Year-Olds: A Personal Journey.* Redmond, WA: Exchange Press.

Hirschland, Deborah. 2015. *When Young Children Need Help: Understanding and Addressing Emotional, Behavioral, and Developmental Challenges.* St. Paul, MN: Redleaf Press.

Hyson, Marilou. 2004. *The Emotional Development of Young Children: Building an Emotion-Centered Curriculum.* New York: Teachers College Press.

Jacobson, Tamar. 1999. "What We Do Matters." *Child Care Information Exchange* Nov. 99: 60–62.

———. 2003. *Confronting Our Discomfort: Clearing the Way for Anti-Bias in Early Childhood.* Portsmouth, NH: Heinemann.

———. 2006. "Resiliency in Children: What We Do Matters." In *Child Development: A Beginnings Workshop Book,* edited by Bonnie Neugebauer. Redmond, WA: Exchange Press.

———. 2008. *"Don't Get So Upset!": Help Young Children Manage Their Feelings by Understanding Your Own.* St. Paul, MN: Redleaf Press.

———. 2010. "Understanding Our Gender Identity: Connecting the Personal with the Professional." Introduction to *Perspectives on Gender in Early Childhood,* edited by Tamar Jacobson, 1–19. St. Paul, MN: Redleaf Press.

———. 2013. "Early education." *Mining Nuggets* (blog), January 2. http://tamarika.typepad.com/mined_nuggets/2013/01/early-education.html.

———. 2016. Child Care Bar and Grill, podcast: www.podcasts.com/child_care_bar_and_grill_podcast/episode/ccbag_0238-tamar-jacobson-2.

Jersild, Arthur T. 1955. *When Teachers Face Themselves.* New York: Teachers College Press.

Karr-Morse, Robin, and Meredith S. Wiley, 1997. *Ghosts from the Nursery: Tracing the Roots of Violence.* New York: Atlantic Monthly Press.

Katz, Lilian. 1995. "Distinctions between Self-Esteem and Narcissism: Implications for Practice." In *Talks with Teachers of Young Children: A Collection.* Norwood, NJ: Ablex Publishing Corporation.

———. 2009. "The Challenges and Dilemmas of Educating Early Childhood Teachers. In *Conversations on Early Childhood Teacher Education: Voices from the Working Forum for Teacher Educators,* edited by Andrew Gibbons and Colin Gibbs. Redmond, WA: World Forum Foundation.

———. 2014. "Standards of Experience." Webinar video, Illinois Early Learning Project, December 2. http://illinoisearlylearning.org/videos/webinars/2014dec-katz.htm.

Kinnell, Gretchen. 2008. *No Biting: Policy and Practice for Toddler Programs.* Second edition. St. Paul, MN: Redleaf Press.

Knapp, Caroline. 2003. *Appetites: Why Women Want.* New York: Counterpoint.

Kohl, Herbert. 2009. *The Herb Kohl Reader: Awakening the Heart of Teaching.* New York: The New Press.

Kohn, Alfie. 1996. *Beyond Discipline: From Compliance to Community.* Alexandria, VA: Association for Supervision and Curriculum Development (ASCD).

Lally, J. Ronald, and Peter Mangione. 2017. "Caring Relationships: The Heart of Early Brain Development." *Young Children* 72, no. 2 (May): 17–24.

Levin, Diane E. 2015. "Compassion Deficit Disorder: What Causes It? What Can We Do about It?" *Community Playthings*, March 3. www.communityplaythings .com/resources/articles/2015/compassion-deficit-disorder.

Lewis, Katherine Reynolds. 2015. "What If Everything You Knew about Disciplining Kids Was Wrong?" *Mother Jones*, July/August. www.motherjones.com /politics/2015/07/schools-behavior-discipline-collaborative-proactive -solutions-ross-greene.

Mangione, Peter. 2017. Keynote address presented at International Infant and Toddler Conference, Tulsa, OK, April 7.

Mead, George Herbert. 1967. *Mind, Self, & Society: From the Standpoint of a Social Behaviorist*. Vol. 1. Edited by Charles W. Morris. Chicago: University of Chicago Press.

McClelland, Megan M., Guadalupe Diaz, and Karley Lewis. 2016. "Self-Regulation." In *The SAGE Encyclopedia of Contemporary Early Childhood Education*, edited by Donna Couchenour and J. Kent Chrisman, 3:1200–1204. Thousand Oaks, CA: SAGE Publications.

Miller, Alice. 2001. *The Truth Will Set You Free: Overcoming Emotional Blindness and Finding Your True Adult Self*. New York: Basic Books.

Murray, Carol Garboden. 2017. Quoted in ExchangeEveryDay, August 4. www .childcareexchange.com/eed/news_print.php?news_id=4459.

National Association for the Education of Young Children (NAEYC). 2017. Hello, Powered by NAEYC, Open Discussion Forum. National Association for the Education of Young Children. http://hello.naeyc.org/communities /community-home/digestviewer?CommunityKey=f51f9fd4-47c9-4bfd -aca7-23e9f31b601e.

Neufeld, Sara. 2015. "Empathy, Not Expulsion, for Preschoolers at Risk." *New York Times*, February 20. https://opinionator.blogs.nytimes.com/2015/02/20 /empathy-not-expulsion-for-preschoolers-at-risk.

Oliver, John. 2015. "Standardized Testing." Video. www.youtube.com /watch?v=J6lyURyVz7k.

Perry, Bruce D. 2007. *Early childhood and Brain Development: How Experience Shapes Child, Community and Culture*. The ChildTrauma Academy. DVD. www.ChildTrauma.org.

———. 2016. "The Brain Science behind Student Trauma: Stress and Trauma Inhibit Students' Ability to Learn." *Education Week*, December 13. www.edweek.org /ew/articles/2016/12/14/the-brain-science-behind-student-trauma.html.

———. 2017. Biography, The ChildTrauma Academy. https://childtrauma.org /wp-content/uploads/2017/02/BDP_Bio_Jan_2017.pdf.

Perry, Bruce D., and Maia Szalavitz. 2006. *The Boy Who Was Raised as a Dog and Other Stories from a Child Psychiatrist's Notebook: What Traumatized Children Can Teach Us about Loss, Love, and Healing*. New York: Basic Books.

Plank, Emily. 2016. *Discovering the Culture of Childhood*. St. Paul, MN: Redleaf Press.

Prinstein, Mitch. 2017. "Popular People Live Longer." *New York Times*, June 1. www .nytimes.com/2017/06/01/opinion/sunday/popular-people-live-longer.html.

Robinson, Sir Ken. 2007. "Do Schools Kill Creativity?" Video, TED Talks Channel, January 6. www.youtube.com/watch?v=iG9CE55wbtY&t=186s.

Rothenberg, Mira. 2002. *Children with Emerald Eyes: Histories of Extraordinary Boys and Girls*. Berkeley, CA: North Atlantic Books.

Rubenstein, Grace. 2017. "Should Emotions Be Taught in Schools?" Ideas.Ted.Com, *We Humans*, February 10. http://ideas.ted.com/should-emotions-be-taught-in-schools.

Searing, Linda. 2017. "Children Whose Parents Spend Time on Mobile Devices Have More Behavior Issues." *Washington Post*, June 10. www.washingtonpost.com/national/health-science/children-whose-parents-spend-time-on-mobile-devices-have-more-behavior-issues/2017/06/09/863f8482-4c6c-11e7-9669-250d0b15f83b_story.html.

Smith, Connie Jo. 2008. *Behavioral Challenges in Early Childhood Settings*. St. Paul, MN: Redleaf Press.

Steinem, Gloria. 1993. *Revolution from Within: A Book of Self-Esteem*. New York: Little, Brown and Company.

Szalavitz, Maia, and Bruce D. Perry. 2010. *Born for Love: Why Empathy Is Essential—and Endangered*. New York: William Morrow.

Thompson, Roger. 2014. "Time's Up for 'Timeout.'" *The Atlantic*, December 19. www.theatlantic.com/education/archive/2014/12/times-up-for-timeout/383897.

Tominey, Shauna L., Elisabeth C. O'Bryon, Susan E. Rivers, and Sharon Shapses. 2017. "Teaching Emotional Intelligence in Early Childhood." *Young Children* 72, no. 1 (March): 6–12.

Tsabary, Shefali. 2010. *The Conscious Parent: Transforming Ourselves, Empowering Our Children*. Vancouver, BC: Namaste Publishing.

UT News. 2016. "Risks of Harm from Spanking Confirmed by Analysis of Five Decades of Research." Press release. University of Texas at Austin, April 25. https://news.utexas.edu/2016/04/25/risks-of-harm-from-spanking-confirmed-by-researchers.

Wayne, Teddy. 2014. "Of Myself I Sing." *New York Times*, August 22. www.nytimes.com/2014/08/24/fashion/of-myself-i-sing.html.

Webb, Jonice. 2014. *Running on Empty: Overcome Your Childhood Emotional Neglect*. New York: Morgan James Publishing.

Wiesel, Elie. 2000. "Oprah Talks to Elie Wiesel." Interview, *O, The Oprah Magazine*. www.oprah.com/omagazine/Oprah-Interviews-Elie-Wiesel/2.

Winnicott, D. W. 1986. *Playing and Reality*. London: Tavistock Publications.

———. 1987. *Home Is Where We Start From: Essays by a Psychoanalyst*. Compiled and edited by Clare Winnicott, Ray Shepherd, and Madeleine Davis. New York: Norton.

Wright Glenn, Amy. 2015. "Screaming to Sleep Part One: The Moral Imperative to End 'Cry It Out.'" *Philly Voice*, January 26. www.phillyvoice.com/screaming-sleep.

Zins, Joseph E., Roger P. Weissberg, Margaret C. Wang, and Herbert J. Walberg, eds. 2004. *Building Academic Success on Social and Emotional Learning: What Does the Research Say?* New York: Teachers College Press.